I'M ~~NOT~~ ENOUGH

How to overcome doubt and reclaim your true value and worth

LEANNE WHITFIELD
Founder Abiding Providence Ministries

REFINERS FIRE PUBLISHING®

© 2022 Leanne Whitfield, First Edition

All rights reserved. No portion of this book may be reproduced, stored in a retrieval system, or transmitted in any form or by any means – electronic, mechanical, photocopy, recording, scanning or other – except for brief quotations in critical reviews or articles, without the prior written permission of the publisher.

Published in Perth Western Australia by Refiners Fire Publishing® PTY LTD.

Scripture quotations are taken from the Holy Bible, New Living Translation, copyright © 1996, 2004, 2015 by Tyndale House Foundation. Used by permission of Tyndale House Publishers, Inc., Carol Stream, Illinois 60188. All rights reserved.

Any internet addresses, phone numbers, or company or product information printed in this book are offered as a resource and are not intended in any way to be or to imply an endorsement by Refiners Fire Publishing®, nor does Refiners Fire Publishing® vouch for the existence, content, or services of these sites, phone numbers, companies, or products beyond the life of this book.

ISBN-13: 978-0-6485832-3-3 (Soft Cover)
ISBN-13:978-0-6485832-4-0 (eBook)

Cover design: of Note Design
Original Cover Photo: Halfpoint, Care of iStock by Getty Images
Author Photo: Choisoul Photography
Interior Design: Glenn Whitfield

Printed in Australia

Dedication

This book is dedicated to my beautiful daughters. Two incredible women oozing with life and talent. I want them to know in the depths of their soul that they are enough. No labels or expectations from others will ever change that. As they live in that truth, they will not only shine their brightest but have peace in their soul.

Chelsea and Georgia, you are the delight of my life and I love doing life with you every day. You are enough, you are loved, and you are incredibly valuable.

I'm Enough

This book is for every person who has not felt...

    pretty enough,

    smart enough,

    tall enough,

    educated enough,

    rich enough,

    talented enough,

    sensitive enough,

    slim enough,

    funny enough,

    diligent enough,

    connected enough,

    wise enough,

    strong enough,

    loud enough,

    passionate enough,

    energetic enough,

    together enough,

    desirable enough,

    valued enough,

    (add yours in here) _____

I'm Enough

Endorsement

"Women across the world struggle with feelings of not being enough. Sometimes we all need to be reminded that we're not alone. In this book, Leanne makes that connection and offers insights about ways of thinking and doing that can change our perspective. And in the process, change our lives."

Kelley Chisholm, Foxglove Project

I'm Enough

Contents

Introduction	1
Chapter One: Eating Leaves	11
Chapter Two: Falling into Crevices	25
Chapter Three: Gym Junkie	37
Chapter Four: Talking to Myself	49
Chapter Five: My Time in the Sunshine	59
Chapter Six: The Addams Family	71
Half Time Chat	82
Chapter Seven: Survival	85
Chapter Eight: Leaving Kids Behind	103
Chapter Nine: Ready, Steady, Go!	119
Chapter Ten: Hearing Voices	135
Chapter Eleven: Sticks and Stones	153
Chapter Twelve: Planning for the Future	165
Conclusion	181
Notes	188

Introduction

I was so excited about my Year 12 high school ball. It was the icing on the cake after many years of hard work at school and it was an opportunity to shine. In the time leading up to the big day we had many conversations between the girls during class and lunch breaks centred around dress colour and style. I spent hours pouring over magazines looking for the "perfect" dress. It was all about the dress! There was something special about this ball that made it significant to me. You see, in Year 11 and we were allowed to attend the Year 12 ball as sort of a practice run. Let's just say it wasn't the fairy tale experience I had imagined!

I'm Enough

To start with, the guy that I was hoping would ask me asked someone else to be his date instead. I then saw all the other possible choices for a date choose girl after girl until I was the one left sitting on the bench. So, what do all self-respecting girls do when they are left on the bench? They pretend they are totally fine with it and that it doesn't hurt to be overlooked and ignored. They pretend that it's a much better idea to go to the ball alone; after all, it's much less complicated that way.

The only topic of conversation that trumped dresses and hairstyles was who everyone was going with. So, for the next few months I employed my best game face and when asked the dreaded question I would confidently say "I am going alone and I'm so happy about it. Think of all the freedom I will be able to enjoy on the night". But inside I was devastated. It was horrible to feel that out of a body of 250 students, nobody wanted to be seen with me.

This reminds me of another "special" moment that I had the pleasure of experiencing in high school when a new guy joined our class and sent the Year 9 girls into meltdown. He was rugged and incredibly handsome, well, as rugged as you can be when you're 15! There was instant competition in the ranks as to which girl would get his attention. When he first entered our social studies class, everyone was already seated and there were very few seats available. As usual, the popular

Introduction

kids, the sporty kids and the bogans were all grouped in their respective areas. For those not familiar with bogans, they wore black skinny jeans, AC/DC or Def Leopard tee-shirts and usually sported a mullet – you get the idea. There was a spare seat up front next to one of the squares. Squares were the studious kids who always got top marks, wouldn't know what a fashion label was and wore glasses. I have nothing against glasses – I wear them myself – but back then, rather than being a fashion statement they signalled that you were probably religious and spent most of your weekends studying at home on your computer. The teacher instructed the Adonis to take a seat and he paused awkwardly; the type of pause that made the whole class pay attention to what would happen next. He exclaimed in rather loud and all too confident voice he would not be sitting next to a square! The entire class erupted into laughter, and although I was a quiet student, I too had a wry smile on my face. Why would he want to sit next to a square? As luck would have it there was also a free seat right next to me which left me thinking, "Suck on that popular girls who always sit together in groups!" The teacher suggested he take the seat next to me and he turned to look at me. Our eyes locked. He had the most incredibly handsome brown eyes that were almost unbearable to look into. Time stood still and the world grew silent in anticipation of his reply. His next words, "I don't want to sit next to her either" were like an arrow going straight through my heart, leaving me utterly devastated. The sound of my classmates erupting into laughter at my expense was absolutely mortifying and I prayed for the ground to swallow me up, right then and there. To make matters worse, the teacher instructed him to take the seat next to me anyway, so I had to endure him for the rest of the class.

Back to my Year 12 Ball...

This year was going to be different and it was my time to shine. What a difference a year makes. I had a steady boyfriend so there was no drama in store for me. He was a year older than me, which really meant something in high school, and was really tall, so eat your heart out Nicole Kidman! I could wear the highest heels without threatening to eclipse him. To add to my delight, I had the perfect dress. As females, we all understand the monumental significance of finding the perfect dress. It was like a dress for a princess and I felt like a million dollars in it. The whole experience was so exciting and in such stark contrast to the previous year when I'd gone to the ball with my friend and her date, only to get stuck looking after him while my friend took off with another guy. Her date didn't go to our school, and because he was lonely

Introduction

I felt bad for him so I spent the night trying to lift his spirits because she had ditched him. Anyyyyhoooow!

This year was a very different story. All the stars aligned and I was walking out of my past and into an exciting future. I had a beautiful dress and a hot boyfriend, who is now my husband (thank me later Glenn), so there was no stress associated with being chosen or not, feeling rejected and worthless or any of those negative feelings. I felt that this was the dawning of a new time for me. As I put on my dress and drove to the ball with Glenn it was like leaving that sense of worthlessness behind and venturing into a whole new world (queue the Aladdin music).

And so my perfect night began. There was great food, wonderful music and lots of fun. As the night was drawing to a close, the organisers announced they would be choosing the beau and belle of the ball, an award given by teachers to the guy and girl who were beautifully dressed and whose behaviour on the night was exemplary and fitting of such an honour. A deafening hush fell over the room as the head of students took the microphone to make the announcement. And then it happened – he called out my name! I was in total shock and wasn't sure I'd heard right. You see, I was Miss Invisible. I'd never won anything and was never the best or the worst. I just flew under the radar where no one noticed me. But now I was the chosen one! It was only when Glenn looked me in the eye and gave me a nudge that I realised I'd heard correctly. I rose to my feet and walked across the dance floor, which seemed incredibly huge and a little more slippery than I remembered as I willed myself not to fall. Eventually, I made it to the podium and received my sash and the most enormous bunch of flowers I have ever received, even to this day (come on Glenn, lift your game!) I could hardly hold them; they were so heavy and unbelievably beautiful.

The white satin sash said in big bold red letters "Belle of the Ball". It marked me as the chosen one, just like Neo in the Matrix, and to say that I felt like a million dollars would be an understatement. I felt like my life was about to change, that I'd gone from an anonymous Miss Average to a blossoming flower, and was in a bubble of euphoria as I marvelled on that evening and reflected on what it meant to me. The presentation was followed by a dance with the chosen beau of the ball, albeit really awkward as I had never even spoken to him before. But soon I was back in Glenn's arms and we were enjoying the night together.

Little did I know that my bubble was about to be burst in the most spectacular fashion. After we finished dancing and made our way back to our table, I found myself surrounded by a group of popular girls. Like a scene out of Mean Girls,

Introduction

they surrounded me and hemmed me in, with the leader closely followed by her sidekicks in true "Mean Girl" style. She stepped towards me and with the confidence and authority of Regina George herself, announced, "You only got Belle of the Ball because they drew the names out of a hat!" It never ceases to amaze me how those girls can utter the most cutting words with a smile on their faces. And there it was. The euphoric bubble that had surrounded me had well and truly burst, and I could feel all those familiar feelings of not being good enough come rushing back.

The mean girl's statement left me feeling that being myself was simply not enough, that being chosen was merely the luck of the draw and had nothing to do with my beauty or exemplary behaviour. At that moment I felt embarrassed and completely worthless. Once the damage was done and they'd achieved their goal, the girls went on their merry way to enjoy the rest of their night.

Have you ever felt that you are not enough? While I may not have a doctorate or multiple best-selling books under my belt, I feel I am more than qualified to talk about not feeling enough. My whole life has been peppered with incidents that have left me feeling not enough. This is an issue that affects each and every one of us in multiple ways and at numerous times in our lives. It can also be the one thing that holds us back from enjoying our lives and living them to the full. The sad truth is that we have all felt this way at various times, whether it was not pretty enough, not popular enough, not skinny enough, not rich enough, not white enough, not intelligent enough or any of the other thousands of "not enoughs". It's a horrible feeling, and I bet you could tell me stories from your life when you also felt you were not enough.

Here's the thing I want you to know. I don't believe it's the way that God intends for us to feel. When I read His word and dwell on His character, it simply does not make sense for us to live our lives feeling worthless and not enough. He chose us before the beginning of time, and the lie that we are not enough and not worthwhile just flies in the face of what God did when He sent His Son to redeem us.

So, in the next few pages we are going to take a journey to understand why we feel this way. Where does this feeling come from? What triggers feelings of not being enough? And what causes us to struggle with seasons of worthlessness? I don't want to leave you with simply understanding; I want you to be encouraged by what you can do about it. How do we face it head-on? How do we walk away from not being enough and embrace our true identity? How do we give the flick to that tormenting feeling of unworthiness that is constantly lurking over our shoulders? How do we avoid

Introduction

the label and go on to being successful in our lives? From chapter 7 we are going to start putting what we have learnt into action using your "I'm Enough" journal. To order your copy, go to www.abidingprovidence.com/shop.

As we go on this journey together, I'm encouraging you to open your heart. Open your heart to God and what He wants to say to you. Engage in the journey and allow those feelings of unworthiness to bubble up and have a voice. Allow the sadness, the pain, the anger and the frustration to come to the surface where God can deal with them and set you free. Allow His truth and His love for you to fill you afresh so that you have everything you need the next time you're faced with the question, "Am I enough?"

Let's begin our journey together.

I'm Enough

Chapter One

Eating Leaves

"If I were given one hour to save the planet, I would spend 59 minutes finding the problem and one minute resolving it."

Albert Einstein

Feeling that you are not enough can be very demoralising. However, once you understand where those feelings are coming from and what triggers them, you can begin to address them head-on. I believe the solution lies in defining the problem. When we identify the types of situations that make us feel like we are not enough, we have access to powerful information that can help us overcome those intensely negative feelings before they take hold. Recognising the triggers means we are empowered to make different decisions in those critical moments. With understanding comes the power to change the choices we make and the way we process situations – and peace in the knowledge that these feelings of worthlessness can be overcome. So, in the next six chapters we will define unworthiness so that we can understand how it invades our lives, and in the six chapters after that, we will discuss ways to overcome it.

I don't remember the day my dad walked out on our family, but the fallout is etched in my memory. I was around 3 years old when he decided to set up home somewhere else and left my mum to raise my brother and me. After he walked out the door, it seemed to me like he never turned back although we did visit with him on weekends and knew he loved us. However, it was never the same as when he lived with us. I don't remember the conversations when my parents decided to separate, nor do I remember how they felt about it, but I remember clearly how I felt. I know it was the day my whole world changed and I went from feeling secure and confident to being part of a broken family that marked me for the rest of my life.

For many years, we were the only single-parent family in our church. Divorce was not as common as it is today and I knew instinctively that we were "different" and somehow "less" than the unbroken families around us. People sympathised with our predicament and felt sorry for us – the poor kids of divorced parents. But despite their pity, everyone seemed to overlook the obvious signs of trauma. I continued to use a dummy for many more years than is socially acceptable and have the dentist bills to prove it! Being away from my mother and my brother sparked deep-seated anxiety in me for fear I would lose them too. This was particularly evident when my mother took me to the shops. Not too far from our house was a big shopping centre called Carousel. Inside, there was a childcare centre where kids were looked after while the adults shopped without distraction. Sounds wonderful, doesn't it? I was not wonderful for a young child suffering from abandonment issues. For me it was absolutely terrifying.

I would cry inconsolably and sometimes succeed in not being left there, but other times my mother would leave and I would be beside myself until she eventually returned. And so it went, week after week. In true 70's style, everything was swept under the rug and life went on, but it felt like I walked with an emotional limp.

Things that happen to us as children can have a huge impact on our lives. They create a lens through which we process events, raise our kids and respond to the world. These events are so significant that it is essential to understand them so that we can live healthy lives. The things that are said and done to us at an early age, especially by people closest to us, such as our parents, siblings, close friends and teachers, impact us in ways that we can wrestle with for the rest of our lives, especially if they are unhealthy relationships. On the flip side, positive experiences are like a firm foundation that sets us on a strong and healthy course for life. It was only when I started counselling to try and unravel the mix of emotions I was struggling with that I began to realise the significance of revisiting and understanding my childhood. This is often the origin of our sense of unworthiness.

Things that happen to us as children can have a huge impact on our lives.

I'm Enough

In the Bible, David is an extraordinary hero. We marvel at his battle victories and learn from his leadership, and we long to be like the man who chased after God's heart. We regard him as someone who had hero status thrust upon him, like Maximus Decimus Meridius in Gladiators, but the reality is that David was not always a hero. In fact, to some he was a pain in the neck. David was a shepherd boy. It seems very biblical and "Jesus-like" to be a shepherd, but reading about this role in ancient times we begin to realise that it was one of the lowliest within the family and not considered the Godly role that we imagine today. As the youngest in the family, David's job was to go out and tend the sheep while his brothers got the more exciting, fulfilling and prestigious roles. We see this play out when Samuel came to anoint one of Jesse's sons to be king and David wasn't even called in from the fields. He wasn't even considered or given a second thought, whereas David's brothers were strapping young men, experienced in battle and the obvious choice to be king. So, right from the start, David was overlooked. I wonder how he felt about that. Did he even notice?

Then we hear about his battle with Goliath. The only reason that David showed up at that battle was to bring food to his brothers and report back to his father on their condition.

Once again, we see David serving in the background. David arrived just in time to witness one of the two daily doses of insults that Goliath served up to the Israelite army who had been cowering in their tents for weeks on end at the sound of the giant's taunts. David came into camp and responded to the giant's insults in a completely unexpected way. I think it's safe to say that David was alarmed by the situation and proceeded to ask questions to try and understand how they got to that point. And all his brothers could do was put him down, because they did not view him as mature enough, wise enough or experienced enough to talk about the situation, let alone face such a formidable foe. But boy, were they wrong.

What you experience as a child is very powerful. Words can sink deep into our hearts and set up home. Events can have a profound impact that never leaves us. David had many things said about him and assumptions made by others that suggested he was not enough and not worth considering. Can you relate? Our response to painful events can impact the decisions we make without us realising it. That's why it is so critical that we stop and take stock of those actions and words.

Our response to painful events can impact the decisions we make without us realising it.

Eating Leaves

Most of us have brothers or sisters. I had an older brother and can remember him shaking his head and looking away in disgust when I didn't do what he wanted me to do. I admired my brother and looked for every opportunity to impress him. On one particular day we were at our dad's house and dad was doing some work in the front garden while we were entertaining ourselves. We started to play "Simon Says", the game where you have to do what someone tells you to if it's preceded by "Simon Says", but if you do what they tell you to without it being preceded by, "Simon Says" then you're out. Only the two of us were playing the game, so it was a pointless exercise, but it passed the time. My brother led the way, picked a leaf off a tree and said, "Simon says eat the leaf." Without even looking up from his gardening, my dad said, "Hey, you're not mucking around with those trees over there, are you?" Silence. My brother and I looked at each other wide-eyed. Those were indeed the trees we had been mucking around with! But what could possibly be harmful about them? Of course, being the perfect little kids that we were, we lied and said, "No, we're not mucking around with those trees." We remained quiet, staring at each other trying to work out what could possibly be dangerous about those trees? Eventually, our curiosity got the better of us and we asked dad, "What would happen if we were to be mucking around with one of those trees?" My dad straightened up and matter-of-factly explained that the leaves of those trees (an Oleander, I later learnt) were extremely poisonous and could make you very, very sick. Translation: death! As I reflect upon it now, even that startling revelation did not shift us into swift action. We paused to contemplate the situation and weigh up our options. We could either confess to dad, get told off and punished for lying, or we could wait and see whether I died! Luckily, we chose the former option and sheepishly confessed to our dad, who dropped his shovel as panic set in. After further questioning he discovered that I had only licked the leaf; nonetheless dad wasn't taking any chances and rushed me off to Princess Margaret Children's hospital for the night. After multiple doses of Ipecac, I was cleared to leave the next morning.

Ahhhh, the power of siblings to make us do just about anything! I wish I could say that was the first and last time I listened to my brother, but it wasn't. Did I mention that he was the cause of most of my childhood injuries? Some people have incredible power to influence us to do all sorts of things. Our need for love and acceptance and feeling worthwhile can be an incredible driving force in our lives, especially when we are young.

Rivalry

Siblings can affect us in another way. Have you experienced sibling rivalry? The competition that goes on between siblings can be very brutal – it often happens when parents aren't around and can be very isolating for the victim. Especially if you are young and inexperienced. Sometimes this rivalry is fuelled by parents who constantly compare us to our siblings and make us feel like we are not enough. Perhaps our siblings got better grades than us, got married earlier or are earning more money than we are. Any number of things can make us feel that we are not enough in our family and constant reminders that we don't measure up can leave us feeling worthless.

Searching for love

Psychologists say that identifying significant experiences in our younger years is critical to unlocking the feelings of unworthiness that we struggle with. When a parent doesn't value our temperament and tries to change us or expects us to perform at a certain level, this causes damage and feeds those feelings of not being enough. Studies have shown that conditional love at an early age is one of the greatest contributors to feelings of unworthiness. The pain comes from being held to the standards of someone who is supposed to love us unconditionally. Perceiving that we are only loved when we do what someone else wants us to do is one of the greatest causes of us feeling unworthy, and it's only when we pause and look back at the pain that we can start walking towards freedom.

Our childhood is a treasure trove of experiences imprinted on our hearts and minds. By becoming aware of what was communicated to us then and processing it with the wisdom of our adulthood now, we can begin to understand where our feelings of unworthiness began. That knowledge is like gold on this journey from worthlessness to true self-worth.

The solution to unworthiness lies in discovering when it first began.

I'm Enough

Chapter Two

Falling into Crevices

"Lies from the enemy,
I am what I have, I am what I do,
I am what other people say or think of me,
I am nothing less than my best moment,
I am nothing more than my worst moment."

Frederick Buechner

I often think about Jesus and the expectations placed on Him. He was born into an average family, hung out with His brothers and learnt the art of carpentry and building. Even though we don't know all of the details, from the outside looking in, it seems that He had a normal, even average life. Then one day Jesus stepped into the Jordan River to be baptised and heaven opened and put on a show. Jesus was the star and the voice of God proclaimed Him as His son. Boy, was that unexpected! Jesus was not what Israel expected after holding out hope for a Saviour for so many years. The Israelites had heard all the prophecies and knew someone was coming. They envisaged a political giant with huge influence or at the very least a military leader with the power and ability to bring about incredible change and freedom to the nation. Once that happened, Israel could then enjoy the fruitful life they had longed for, free from Roman oppression. They would own their land and live in freedom in the way God had intended. In comparison to what they expected, Jesus would have been a huge disappointment. What was this carpenter's son going to do? Shoot the Romans with His nail gun?

To their surprise peculiar things started to happen when Jesus was around. Water was turned into wine, people were healed, some were raised from the dead and even demons listened to Him. Jesus was not what they expected, which caused them to be confused and disappointed. The irony here is that they were disappointed that He wasn't what they wanted, yet He gave them more than they could ever have dreamed of. Israel expected someone who would give them freedom on earth, whereas Jesus came to die for their everyone's salvation for all eternity. Jesus offered so much more than they expected, yet they were disappointed.

Have you ever felt that people are disappointed in you? The belief that we are what society says we are is a nasty trap to be caught in. It places control in the hands of others and we are at their mercy. There are always going to be people in our lives that influence and impact us. It is up to us to decide who those people are and how much influence they have. Too often we substitute what we feel or think with someone else's opinion because we consider them greater or more experienced than us. When we put people on pedestals and substitute our own thoughts for theirs it's very easy to fall into the trap of feeling like we're not enough when we don't meet their expectations.

Too often we substitute what we feel or think with someone else's opinion because we consider them to be wiser or more experienced than us.

Falling into Crevices

In the previous chapter, we talked about childhood hurt and the experiences that shape us when we are young. I have already mentioned that my brother had a huge impact on my life. We grew up at a time before computer games and mobile phones so when we went to visit someone we created our own fun and entertainment. I use the word "fun" loosely because most of the time it resulted in me getting hurt! Our entertainment involved activities like trespassing in the neighbour's yard, drawing on apartment walls with charcoal and throwing rocks at cars. Harmless stuff like that!

On one particular day, we went to a house in the hills with our mum. It was a beautiful property nestled on the side of the hill. The view over the valley and orchards was truly something to behold. As mum settled in for a cup of tea with her friends, we went off in search of "entertainment" for ourselves. It didn't take long for my brother to clamber up the hill and jump on a water tank built into the side of the hill, from where we had the most spectacular view of the valley. It was also a great vantage point to see how far we could ditch rocks down the valley. We finished playing and it was time to get down. Getting on the water tank was effortless, but getting off was a different story. The slope of the roof was steeper than it looked from my original vantage point and the galvanized metal was more slippery too. To make matters worse, there was a large trench around the tank which meant there was a gap between the top of the tank and the ledge we had to jump to. I was terrified, so I did this butt-slide thing that took me as close as possible to the edge. As I peered over, the trench was not only wider but a whole lot deeper than I anticipated. Fear and panic set in as I envisaged being on this water tank for the rest of my life. People would have to throw me food parcels and I would have to sew suction cups onto my pillow to keep it in place as I slept. And how would Santa deliver my Christmas presents without a chimney?

Time passed while I procrastinated and my brother became increasingly agitated. He tried all sorts of ways to get me to jump, but nothing worked. Eventually, he lost patience with me and I remember a look of complete and utter disgust on his face. Those of us with older siblings know only too well that look of disappointment when we fail to meet their expectations. After what seemed like ages he said, "Fine! I will go and get mum" and started to walk off. I knew I had let him down, when all I wanted was to be the cool little sister, not a drag. I wanted to be the one he bragged about to his friends, not the one he tried to disown. All these feelings of not being enough in his eyes swirled around in my mind and suddenly the fear of not being enough outweighed the peril of the jump. I summoned every ounce of courage and jumped. Like a gazelle, I soared through the air with ease and landed gracefully on the other side. Greeted in my brothers open arms he hoisting me up into the air with triumphant shouts of joy! Well... that's what I wish had happened! But I was sadly mistaken. I jumped, fell straight into the trench, banging my arm on the edge as I went down. Not only was my arm fractured but my pride also. On the upside, my brother drew a great picture of Wonder Woman on my plaster cast!

Expectations are really powerful. The expectations of others can drive us to impress them and do things that we wouldn't normally do. Subconsciously, they exert a powerful impact and coerce us into pleasing others so that we feel worthwhile. If we live our lives trying to meet everyone else's expectations we are never going to be at peace with who God created us to be. Instead, we'll live in fear of having to be something more or being what others have labelled us. When we value the expectations of others beyond everything else we live inauthentic lives, dismissive

If we live our lives trying to meet everyone else's expectations we are never going to be at peace with who God created us to be.

of who we were created to be, and all the while, the failure to meet those expectations continue to perpetuate feelings of not being good enough.

The advent of social media has created high expectations of people. As we trawl through social media we see highlights of everyone's lives and only the best photos and the most noteworthy experiences are there for the world to see. I have yet to see a photograph of someone first thing in the morning, cleaning a toilet or scrubbing a floor. Most social media portray people's best moments that we view from the perspective of our reality, sitting there in our pyjamas with crazy hair after a rotten day. No wonder we don't feel good enough when we look at glamorous bikini shots in Bali, glitzy new cars and fun catch-ups with friends. What we're saying to ourselves is "I'm not fun enough, I'm not pretty enough, my body is not good enough, I'm not successful enough, I don't have enough friends, my life is not exciting enough, I'm not popular enough". We feel like everyone is out there having fun except us and don't get me started on "likes" and "comments"! I hardly post anything on social media other than my ministry info, because like many others, I think my life is not exciting or interesting enough for anyone to want to know about. I've often been tempted to put up photos, but then been put off by thoughts like "I don't look good enough" or "it isn't a good enough photo" or "it's not artistic enough". Arrrgggghhh! The pressure of expectations!

Society will always have expectations of us. The problem is they keep changing. What was socially acceptable five years ago is no longer so. Believe it or not, high-volume permed hair was actually in fashion once upon a time and there are photos from the 80s to prove it! But now, sleek soft curls are the fashionable norm. If we hold society's expectations in high esteem we will continually be chasing one acceptable convention after another and lose sight of our authentic selves. The myths that we buy into are also damaging. Advertisements that promise transformations in 10 days or in 5 easy steps are just not practical or helpful. When we buy into these illusions we are destined to fail and wind up feeling not enough, just as comparing our realities with other people's Facebook and Instagram leave us feeling envious and falling short. Social activities that engage us in making a contribution are far more beneficial, because they not only connect us, but also encourage positive well-being.

Looking for value and worth outside of ourselves is short-lived because the world is always changing. What was "cool" and "in" yesterday is no longer so today. Hitching our wagon to that kind of validation is an empty way to live, not to mention exhausting.

Our time and energy are far better spent looking at what's on the inside and growing and developing that part of ourselves. That is where we will find our true value.

I'm Enough

Chapter Three

Gym Junkie

> *"Confidence is not, they will like me.
> Confidence is, I'll be fine if they don't."*
>
> *Christina Grimme*

I'm Enough

After I had my first set of twins I realised that I loved going to the gym and getting fit. It was a great opportunity to get out of the house and meet people while staying fit and healthy. I eventually turned that passion into a personal training qualification. I was learning Taekwondo and training five to six days a week at my gym to achieve my goal of competing in a fitness figure competition. I had been training hard and began to diet down two months before the fitness figure competition. Dieting down is a process of limiting your food intake so that the body is in its best condition to show muscle development to the judges. It was a fine line of drastic calorie reduction versus not losing too much muscle mass. Needless to say, it was a complicated task.

It had been four years since our boys had been born and we were thinking about having another child. Because it was so difficult to fall pregnant the first time around, we were under no illusions that this time would be any different, and to make matters worse, three doctors had told us we would never fall pregnant again without some type of medical assistance. We weren't as desperate this time and decided not to do another round of IVF, concluding that if the boys were all the offspring we would have then we were very blessed indeed. I went off the pill fully expecting nothing to happen, but it did. I fell pregnant that same month, and to our amazement we discovered that we were having a second set of twins.

My doctor struggled to understand this absolute miracle. My dieting stopped and I began to prepare for the upcoming birth. My eating changed drastically; from chicken and lettuce to chocolate and coke. I kept up my training and, by the final few weeks I could barely wrap my Taekwondo belt around my waist even though it usually wrapped around me twice. After our twin girls were born I realised that the chocolate and Coca-Cola had taken a toll and I had put on more weight in my second pregnancy than my first. Although I had exercised, I was struggling to get back to my pre-pregnancy weight, and when I returned to work, it was not in the same peak condition in which I had left. But I knew it was early days and things would change.

Soon after the girls were born I started personal training again, but at different times from usual. Normally I hung out with the morning crowd, which was mainly mums who would arrive after they dropped their kids off at school. There's something about us moms. We're forgiving of each other and we understand how hard it is to be a mum and keep up this perfect body image, so we always gave each other a bit of slack.

After coming back to work I was training a couple of people in the evening when males typically dominated the gym. I could smell the testosterone as I opened the door and all eyes were upon us as we trained. On this occasion, a very fit European man in his 60s came up to me while I was training my client and told me that I should not be training anyone looking like I did! I wish I could tell you that I gave him a witty response that put him in his place, but just like with the mean social-studies-guy, I wished the ground would swallow me up. Being an introverted person who needs time to go away and process things before responding just doesn't help in situations like this. I was completely shocked and embarrassed and really intimidated by this man's words. I'd never spoken to this man before, yet he felt confident to judge me, and in the face of my pathetic two-year-old response, "Well, I just had my second set of twins", he just snorted and walked off. To add insult to injury, he proceeded to critique me every time I came in to train a client. His words really spoke to my vulnerabilities at the time. I knew I wasn't in the condition I wanted to be in, and the truth is I was upset with myself because I had trained so hard right up to my pregnancy and then just let myself go.

I was struggling to adjust from having two kids to four and keeping it all together, not to mention breastfeeding for six months, which is quite a feat with twins! In all the chaos, getting my body back into shape just wasn't a priority, caring for myself had taken a back seat and this man had made me feel very, very uncomfortable.

The Intimidation Barrier

Have you ever felt intimidated by someone and so affected by their presence that you just aren't yourself? Your confidence and self-worth vanish and a fear sets in that grips hold and stops you from moving forward. Intimidation can really disarm and hold us back because it makes us feel worthless. When I look at Scripture, there are so many examples of intimidation affecting people's lives. Gideon is by far the example I relate to the most. He's the guy in the Old Testament that was born at a tumultuous time in Israel's history when Israel was being horribly oppressed by their enemies.

I'm Enough

When we meet Gideon for the first time he is hiding in a winepress. That probably doesn't sound all that strange until we discover that Gideon is trying to thresh wheat. Now, I'm no farmer, but from my extensive research into farming techniques in biblical times (you're worried now, aren't you!) I know that threshing wheat is supposed to happen in an open airy space so that the wind removes the husk and leaves the grain.

Gideon was threshing his wheat in the wine press because he was intimidated by his enemy and desperate to survive. He was probably also starving and managed to find a space that was hidden away so that no one could see him thresh his wheat and prepare it for his family.

It's interesting how intimidation can cause us to hide away and do things in a way that we wouldn't normally do. Take Elijah as an example. He comes off an incredible showdown with the prophets of Baal, where the fire of God rains down and makes the prophets look like complete turkeys, showing Elijah's God, the God of Israel to be supreme. But then Miss Meanie, Queen Jezebel, gets wind of the situation and threatens to obliterate Elijah. Rather than boasting about what his God can do,

Intimidation can really disarm and hold us back because it makes us feel worthless.

I'm Enough

Elijah runs off into the desert and hopes to die. What an extreme contrast. That is what intimidation can do, it will take you from the heights of confidence to the depths of despair... if you allow it. What we need to understand is that intimidation is a spirit at work. Have you over come across someone who immediately intimidates you? They may not have said anything and you may never have met them before, but your confidence drains away and you feel intimidated. The spirit of intimidation is powerful and it makes you feel powerless and small.

As Gideon threshed his wheat, thinking he was safe and hidden from the world, the angel of the Lord decided to pay him a visit. The angel spoke loudly and confidently. Gideon was in his hiding place where he felt safe and secure when along came an angel of radiant light, threatening to give away his position. The angel spoke the words we all wish were true when we are hiding in our wine presses feeling intimidated, "Stand up good and mighty warrior!" I wonder if Gideon suppressed a smile at the irony of being called a mighty warrior while clearly cowering in the shadows?

Gideon was completely intimidated. He was doing something that was out of place while hiding away from the meanies, yet an angel came and called him a mighty warrior. At that point he felt nothing at all like a mighty warrior. Intimidation caused him to feel anything but the man that God had called him to be. Intimidation can have the same effect on us all, causing us to hide away from who we are and what we are called to do. Intimidation screams to us that we are not enough and we believe it. Irrespective of how Gideon felt, God's declaration let him know that he was a mighty warrior and nothing or nobody could change that. All Gideon had to do was dare to believe it. Gideon trusted God and became part of His rescue plan for the nation of Israel, but the story gets even crazier before that happens, so it's definitely worth a read!

There may be people in your world right now that make you feel intimidated when you're around them. Keep in mind that intimidation comes from our perceptions of a person and not necessarily from their behaviour. When we perceive them as powerful or better than us, we shrink away from our calling because we don't feel good enough. In his book, Breaking Intimidation, which

I highly recommend if anything I'm talking about is resonating with you, John Bevere says, "What we do not confront will not change". We need to confront the spirit of intimidation that is operating in our lives to recognise it when it comes and deal with it.

Intimidation is a spiritual attack, grounded in fear of man. If we do not recognise this spiritual attack in our lives we will continue to battle with it for years. And worse than battling with things for a day is battling with them for years when we can actually do something about it. But it all starts with learning to recognise intimidation and how it makes us feel "not enough".

Intimidation is a spiritual attack, grounded in fear of man.

I'm Enough

Chapter Four

Talking to Myself

> "A man is but the product of his thoughts,
> what he thinks, he becomes."
>
> *Mahatma Gandhi*

I'm Enough

One day I woke up to find my whole world had changed. There was a very dark cloud in my mind that just wouldn't go away. Like Eeyore in Winnie the Pooh, I was going through life with a dark cloud following me everywhere I went. I couldn't escape it. When I went to bed it was there and when I woke up in the morning it was still there. Up until this point I had never experienced depression before. Friends and family had suffered from it, but like most things, I never truly understood how debilitating it was until I experienced it for myself. I did some research on Dr Google, desperately trying to find a way to make it go away, and hung on to every word that others said about depression, asking them endless questions.

The first thing that surprised me was how easy it arrived. I wish I could credit its genesis to some big event, but I literally went to bed, as usual, one night and woke up a different person. The second thing that shocked me was how disconnected I felt from my old self as if that version of Leanne had been left behind The thought that she might never return really scared me. Feeling like we have changed into a new person can be a good thing when the change makes us wiser and stronger, but this was not a welcome change or a wonderful thing. I wanted the old Leanne back. I hated the person who had unexpectedly moved in and was terrified that she was here to stay. To say that depression is a dark place is an understatement. The conversation that went on in my head at those times was filled with hopelessness and pain.

Our thoughts are powerful and sometimes our thinking goes unchecked. How often do we take stock of our thoughts and what we feel about ourselves? If we were to write down the billions of thoughts that we have during a day, I wonder what we would learn about ourselves? How many of those thoughts would be positive, encouraging and uplifting, and how many of them would be hateful, mean and self-deprecating? Could our own thoughts contribute to feelings of being not enough? Moses is a classic example of someone who struggled with who he was and who he was called to be. One day, God caught Moses' attention in the form of a burning bush and told him he would bring the entire Israelite nation out of captivity. Make no mistake, this was an incredibly big job and an awesome privilege for Moses to be called by God to lead this amazing rescue. God knew He had equipped Moses with everything he needed to fulfil the task if only Moses trusted in Him. Yet Moses had quite a different opinion. We read about how he argued with God, laying out all his insecurities and shortcomings. He told God all the things he couldn't do and how he wasn't up to the job. Whether it was because he stuttered when he spoke, had no title or position of authority or was not an extraction expert, Moses thought of himself as just an average guy. Not to mention that 40 years earlier Moses had killed an Egyptian and hid the body, which caused him to flee into the desert when it was later discovered. I can understand why Moses didn't feel up to God's proposal. I also wonder how much his thoughts and doubts played into his insecurities about fulfilling God's calling. I wonder what words he said to himself that nobody else heard?

It's interesting the power that words have in our lives. In chapters one and two we talked about the words that other people speak of us, but what about the words that we speak to ourselves and the words that no one else hears and knows about? What about the words we speak to ourselves when we wake up in the middle of the nigh and the questions we ask ourselves about what we're doing and where we're going? How healthy are those words in our lives? We've all experienced people saying hurtful things to us. The truth is that we sometimes continue to repeat those words to ourselves long after those people have disappeared from our lives. I remember a phrase that was spoken to me when I was growing up, "Don't worry, you're just dumb, so don't try to do anything because you're just going to fail and be disappointed". It may have only been said a few times, but it was enough to lodge deep in my heart and remain there. From that point on I didn't need to hear it from someone else because I was saying it to myself every time I faced something new or challenging. Those thoughts would flood my mind, "I'm not smart enough to do that or don't bother trying because I'm going to fail".

According to psychologists, after thinking something for an extended period of time the thoughts become automatic and we stop questioning whether they're right or wrong. Recently I did a test that takes you through a series of questions to identify your personal leadership strengths and was shocked to learn that one of my top five strengths is intelligence. As I read the results all those feelings of not being intelligent enough came to the surface and I actually felt irritated, thinking the results were wrong. It reminded me how powerful the tapes are that play in our heads 24/7. When I thought I had dealt with the issue and put it to bed, there was apparently still a remnant of the belief that I was not smart enough.

Negative self-talk is one of the biggest contributors to not feeling enough. It's like a silent assassin, invisible to other people who don't know we're doing it. Imagine if you had a friend who said all the things to themselves that you secretly say to yourself. You would be shocked? Would it break your heart to know the filth and rubbish, not to mention the lies, that they pored over day after day? As a good friend, you wouldn't stand for it. You would challenge that rubbish with the truth and compel your friend to change their thoughts. If that is the case with our friends why aren't we kinder to ourselves? After all, we have to live with ourselves all the time. We think it's okay, but it's not okay.

Negative self-talk is insidious because it erodes us from the inside out with feelings of worthlessness and not being enough. It says that we are not smart enough, pretty enough, popular enough, successful enough, tall enough or skinny enough. All these thoughts swirl around in our minds, and for the most part, no one around us is even aware that it's going on. Negative self-talk destroys our joy and holds us in a place of not feeling enough.

Studies show there are different levels of belief. There is an automatic belief about something, like when a thought pops into our head. Then there are underlying assumptions that we make about the things that happen around us. They are the beliefs that guide how we navigate the world. Finally, there are our core beliefs. They come in pairs and we either believe one or the other. For example, "I'm not good enough" is a core belief that contradicts the belief that, "I am good enough."

Negative self-talk is insidious, because it erodes us from the inside out with feelings of worthlessness and not being enough.

When negative core beliefs are stronger than positive ones, we struggle with feelings of worthlessness. They are extremely powerful and become entrenched in our psyches. When they remain negative, feelings of unworthiness seep into our lives and trap us in a cycle.

I wonder what thoughts are swirling around in your head? Are they positive or downright damaging? If you were to write down every thought that came into your head today, how many of them would be positive and how many of them would be negative? That is what we're feeding our brains and that's how we're living our lives. The thoughts that we collect day by day and live with all the time determine how we see ourselves and the world around us.

Continuing to feed and indulge negative thoughts will continue to breed feelings of unworthiness and being not enough.

It is a sobering thought that we become what we believe. I have a saying written on my bathroom mirror that says, "Whatever you think about the most, grows". I keep it there because I never want to become complacent about the thoughts that fill my mind, and the power they have to determine my destiny.

Words have power in

our lives.

I'm Enough

Chapter Five

My Time in the Sunshine

"I am I not pretty enough?"

Kasey Chambers

I'm Enough

"Not Pretty Enough" is a song written by country music star Kasey Chambers in response to feeling inferior in the superficial music industry. Written in 2001 she saw people like Brittney Spears, Shakira and Christina Aguilera attaining fame and popularity and felt like she didn't fit in. As an accomplished singer and songwriter, who had won numerous ARIA awards, said confessed she spent a lot of time not feeling pretty enough when she compared herself to others. How sad is that? Comparing ourselves to others is a slippery slope that quickly leads us down the path of not feeling good enough.

When I was in school, our teacher gave us an incentive. If we did well and behaved he would take us out on his catamaran. I had never been on a catamaran before, so the prospect was very exciting. Every fortnight he chose six students to accompany him out on the water for a day of sailing, and on Friday afternoons we would all eagerly wait for our names to be called out. I didn't get picked the first week, and although I was disappointed, I wasn't surprised. I knew where I was in the classroom pecking order, right in the middle. I was not the best or brightest student, but I also wasn't one of the naughty ones, so it came as no surprise to me that the

Comparing ourselves to others is a slippery slope that quickly leads us down the path of not feeling good enough.

popular, charismatic students got chosen first. That's the way it goes, doesn't it?

Just a side note to any teachers out there. The students in your class who fly under the radar may not be the smartest or most charismatic, but they also don't give you a hard time and turn your hair grey. They show up day after day and try their best, knowing they're not the smartest, but that doesn't mean they aren't giving it all they've got. They get unfairly punished along with the naughty kids as if punishing the whole class will somehow stir the conscience of the naughty ones and cause them to turn over a new leaf and change their behaviour. Just so you know, it doesn't work! The kids who fly under the radar are valuable and want to be noticed. Even a simple kind, encouraging word will do. Acknowledging them and letting them know you value them, even once, will make a huge impact on their lives. Just a suggestion. It's probably no surprise that I chose to home-school my kids, given all my hang-ups with experiences with school!

But back to the sailing. The hurt started when the naughty students got chosen to go on the boat before me. I was an angel compared to them, so why hadn't I been chosen? It seemed to me they behaved themselves for one day and the reward was theirs. I sat there thinking "What about me?

Was I not good enough to get my teacher's attention?" As the weeks passed and I didn't get chosen, my feelings of not being enough grew larger. Then it was the last week of term and only one weekend left, so the teacher scanned his list and saw there were four kids who hadn't yet been invited, me being one of them. By default, we were chosen to go boating that last week and I felt completely deflated. It was more like a consolation prize than something I'd earned, and I remember being absolutely gutted and hurt that the popular kids and the naughty kids were chosen ahead of me. I felt like an afterthought, and feelings of not being enough swirled around inside me and held me captive.

Comparison is a really powerful thing, isn't it? When we encounter hard times and everyone around us seems to be experiencing the opposite, it seems like they are clearly hearing from God, having doors opened for them and God's favour consigned on them. They appear to be excelling in their personal lives and flourishing in their spiritual journeys, and by comparison, we feel overlooked. I've often felt like the person holding the door open for others to go through and have their dreams realised. I have supported, helped and encouraged others to reach their dreams, all the while wondering when is my time in the sunshine?

I'm Enough

My kids loved the movie Shrek, and about 15 years ago we had a DVD of the movie. If you don't know what a DVD is, just ask your parents. The first screen that comes up is a picture of all the characters in the movie gathered together. There are a lot of storybook characters in the movie so it's quite a crowd, but at the back of the crowd one can see a donkey's head as he jumps up and down, hoping to get noticed. I find myself feeling deep empathy and affection for this donkey as he jumps up and down saying "pick me, pick me!" Sometimes I feel like that donkey. I blend in with the crowd, hoping to be chosen for something big, but am constantly swamped by the crowd.

It reminds me of an interesting time when I was pregnant. Something crazy happens to us when we're pregnant, and if you're not aware it can catch you completely off guard. Let me give you an example. People feel it's totally appropriate to come up and touch your stomach when you're pregnant. I am yet to have a person come up and stroke my stomach when I'm not pregnant, but for some absurd reason, the fact that my stomach is rapidly expanding like Sigourney Weaver's in Alien seems to give total strangers permission to touch it. I wonder if men with beer bellies experience the same thing.

And don't get me started on the inappropriate comments that come out of their mouths!

Let me share another experience with you. A frequent comment I encountered when I was pregnant was, "you're so huge!" Now I ask you, when is it ever okay to make that statement? I really can't think of any scenario that makes it okay to say that to someone. When does a woman feel uplifted and encouraged to receive those words? Perhaps if you were referring to a hippo at the zoo or a Baskin and Robbins super-sized milkshake, but never in reference to a person. Come on meanies, think! My rehearsed response to that statement would be, "Well I am having twins" (remember I'm not gifted at witty response). Sharing that revelation would be met with "Oh, you're not very big at all." Are you kidding me? I went from being scouted for the next Goodyear Blimp to being under-sized for carrying twins! What people think is okay to say when you're pregnant completely astounds me.

Unfortunately, as women, judgement and comparisons are not confined to when we are pregnant. Pretty much all our lives we're subjected to society's expectations of who we should be as women. Every billboard, poster, magazine and TV advertisement paint a picture of the "ideal" woman, so it's no wonder the comparison trap is such a huge contributing factor to not feeling good enough. The need to compare starts at an early age. Siblings compare food, commenting that someone else got a bigger piece of cake or a bigger glass of fizzy drink. Christmas becomes a competition about who got more presents. And when you add the "twin factor", the comparison game reaches new heights. We've always treated all our kids as individuals. They were very different from birth and so we tried not to turn them into pigeon pairs, but rather embrace their uniquely individual personalities. You would think this would have earned us the "Best Parents" award, but sadly, no. I've lost count of the number of times I've brought home something special for one of them and the other has been offended because they didn't get the same. "Well Johnny, (not their actual names to protect their identity) Ben is into football and you're not, so why would I buy you 10 sets of football collector cards?"

Psychologists say at the age that a child begins schooling their problem-solving development begins. They start to notice they are not the best at everything and there are others in the class that are smarter or more popular or can colour in better than they can. This is where comparisons begin to leave us feeling that we are not enough. We learn that someone else is faster and gets the blue ribbon, however nowadays everyone seems to get a ribbon, whether you come first or last. The truth is there's always going to be someone who's faster, smarter, more popular or has more money than us. Very few people can claim to be the best in the world for something, it is a very elite and limited minority. Even then they can usually only claim to be the best in one specific area and for a limited time. I am yet to meet someone who is number one in every area of life. We need to stop comparing and start being the star of our own story because comparisons leave us feeling defeated, destroyed and not good enough.

The Bible contains several stories about comparison. Cain and Abel, Jacob and Esau. Even the disciples argued about who was the greatest. But by far the most profound story of comparison opens the Bible, with devastating repercussions. Adam and Eve are the only ones in the luscious garden of Eden, surrounded by extraordinary fruit and flowers and a variety of amazing animals. Well, all except one, the serpent that didn't have Adam and Eve's best interests at heart. One sunny day, this serpent slithered into their lives and changed it forever in the simplest of ways. Comparison. He started with a question that raised doubt in Eve's heart, "Did God say you could not eat of this tree in the garden?" After

We need to stop comparing and start being the star of our own story.

sowing the seeds of doubt with his question he cleverly followed up with, "If you eat from this tree you will become as wise as God knowing good from evil." For the first time Eve became aware that there was someone greater than her, someone who knew more than her, and that someone was God. With heightened awareness of her shortcomings and an overwhelming desire to be like God, she made the same decision that all rebellious children make. Just like Nemo and Moana who disregarded their parents' instructions and went their own way, Eve made the fateful decision to eat the fruit. Adam and Eve's eyes were opened by a revelation, but not the one they expected. Their revelation was that they were not enough in their desire to be like God and they discovered painfully just how different they were.

In the news, we often see how comparisons and jealousy have caused people to make tragic decisions with devastating results. Although we may not have experienced the same kind of tragedy, we still feel the impact and pain of comparison and how it can debilitate us and keep us trapped in feelings of not being enough.

I'm Enough

Chapter Six

The Addams Family

"There is no fear like the fear of being found out."

Unknown author

I'm Enough

If there was one disciple that I relate to and admire most, it would have to be Peter. His relationship with Jesus had its ups and downs and reflects my own relationship with God. Peter is like my kindred spirit. We read about Jesus walking on water in Matthew 14, and Peter asking if he can come out onto the water with Jesus. Peter was excited to do that. He had courage and tenacity. Sometimes I feel that way too and want to step out into unknown waters. The thrill is so exciting to me. But then there's also reality. When Peter began to comprehend what he was doing, fear set in and he began to sink As the water level rose around him, he took his focus off Jesus and lost faith. As he sank beneath the water terrified, Jesus reached out and saved him. I get how Peter felt. Sometimes stepping out into the unknown is so exciting, but when we're actually out there, fear begins to seep in and we wonder what in the world were we thinking?

A short time later the transformation took place, the event on top of the mountain where only Peter, James and John were with Jesus. As they were standing around, Jesus' appearance suddenly changed and he became like a human light bulb. Then Elijah and Moses appeared for a chat. It must have been an incredible thing to witness and probably left those disciples in absolute awe. Shortly afterwards Jesus asked the disciples, "Who do you say that I am?" And Peter boldly answered, "You are the Messiah, the Son of the living God". Way to go Pete! He was the only one to respond and Jesus was happy with Peter's answer. Jesus blessed him, changed his name to Peter, meaning rock, proclaimed Peter would be fundamental to building His church and that it would be successful. What a fantastic promise for Peter to hold on to.

There have been moments in my life when I have been bold. I felt invincible as I served the Lord and did things that I never thought I would. It's such a great feeling to know that you are fearlessly following God, knowing that you are stepping out into areas you've never been before and having success. And then there are the moments where I've felt that I'm falling short. We see this happen to Peter a short while later. Jesus talked about His death to His disciples and explained to them what was going to happen, but Peter wouldn't hear of it. He stood up and boldly reprimanded Jesus with words like, "Heaven forbid it, Lord, that this will ever happen to You", to which Jesus replied, "Away from me satan." Wow, what a stinger! The guy who seemed to be Jesus' favourite and was promised the world was now being referred to as satan. It seemed like Peter couldn't win. I don't know about you, but I find God somewhat mysterious. He's a little bit scary and I'm not always sure what He's thinking. If I'd lived in Jesus' day, I don't think I would have been His best friend. I would have been wary of Him because He said and did things that were really unpredictable. Just when I thought I had a handle on Him and was in His good books I would inevitably say something that disappointed Him. He was just so unpredictable, and I see this same struggle in Peter's relationship with Him.

But there's more, and we progress to a conversation Jesus had with Peter just before He is taken away to be crucified. Jesus reveals to Peter that he is going to deny Jesus. How gut-wrenching that must have been. It was so offensive to Peter that he instantly defended himself. However after Jesus crucifixion he was approached by different people and his fear of being linked to Jesus caused him to deny ever knowing Him, not once, not twice, but three times.

There have been times in my life when I've told God that I will never deny him. I've felt so confident and clear that the thought of rejecting Him seemed utterly ridiculous to me. Yet there have been times when I haven't spoken up, haven't done what He asked and out of fear done exactly what Peter did. I can totally relate to Peter's devastation when that cock crows and he realises what he has done. Even simple things, like committing to a regular time of prayer and Bible reading can be easily disrupted by the most unimportant distractions and I find myself completely off track.

Fear has a huge impact on our lives. It makes us do things we don't want to do and stops us from doing things we want to do. Fear can impact us so much that we lose our confidence in who we are and walk away from what we are called to do. When I was growing up, we lived just around the corner from my school. Every year in the week before school resumed, staff attached a class list to the office window that told us what class we were in and which teacher we had. As the Christmas holidays drew to a close we took daily walks to school to see whether the list had been put up. The trip was filled with a mixture of anxiety and excitement. We wanted to know who our teacher was and which friends were in our class, but there was also a certain fear that we wouldn't get a teacher we liked or that we would be separated from our friends. Fortunately, there were only a few teachers we didn't like. For me, there was really only one I dreaded, Mrs. Allen. What were the chances of me getting that one awful teacher? Apparently, very high! As I looked at the list for my Grade 4 class fear and dread washed over me all at once as I saw Mrs. Allen's name. This totally destroyed the last few days of my holidays as I went into a deep anxiety that continued for the rest of the year. I was absolutely terrified of her.

Fear can impact us so much that we lose our confidence in who we are and walk away from what we are called to do.

The Addams Family

We had a tradition in our house that if we got ready for school on time we were allowed to watch TV. It's incredible how sounds and smells from certain times of your life become ingrained in your memory, sometimes with good connotations and sometimes bad, to the point where they immediately transport you back to that time and place. That's how it was with me and the Addams family. To this day, the sound of that music and clicking fingers make my stomach tighten. "Dunnaduna, click, click, dunnaduna, click, click, dunnaduna, dunnaduna, dunnaduna, click, click" (the interpretation is mine – Google doesn't spell it out, unfortunately). The song affects me so much that I've never allowed my kids to watch it. I've loved introducing them to the Brady Bunch, which in my opinion is the best kids' series ever, but the Addams family is entirely different, being the last show that I could watch before going to school. At the sound of "dunnaduna, click, click" my pulse would race, tears would well up in my eyes and a sick feeling washed over me. I'd usually end up crying in the laundry where my mum was ironing, pleading with her not to have to go.

For Mrs Allen, school was not a nurturing, learning environment. It was a sport, and humiliation was her number one weapon of choice. She ran her classroom with military precision and you didn't dare break the rules. To those of us who fly under the radar, the thought of being singled out by her was terrifying. If we weren't paying attention, she threw chalk at us. If there was a fart smell in the room, she would spray us with air freshener while belittling us. But by far her biggest thrill was singling out kids for public humiliation with a gleam in her eye.

One day we were learning about rounding in maths. At one point she asked if anyone would come up to the board and round a particular number. While I'm not usually one to put my hand up, I felt that I had grasped the concept of rounding and for some totally absurd reason, put my hand up to answer. Let me clarify for a moment, I put my hand up to about shoulder height very gingerly. Immediately Mrs Allen's eyes widened in delight. You see, she was particularly venomous towards me, perhaps because my mother had told her I was terrified of her, and rather than helping the situation she seemed to take more delight in tormenting me. It may also have been because my friends and I were outside her classroom window one day laughing about her hairy legs without realising the window was open and she could hear us. Or the time I vomited all over my school desk because I was too scared to leave the room without her permission. Perhaps she was just a nasty woman who should have retired years ago. Either way, she had a glint of delight in her eyes as my hand went up and immediately invited me to the front of the class for the humiliation to begin. In my heart of hearts I knew the answer, but alas, I got it wrong, rounding up when I should have rounded down. As the smile formed on her face I could feel the blood draining out of my head. Why did I put myself out there? I should have just stayed silent at the back of the class. Who cares about rounding anyway? I can honestly say it's a skill I've rarely had to use.

She called me over and told me to bend over in front of the class. The humiliation was about to begin. Standing beside me and with great delight she took some practice swings at my butt. Now as alarming as this scenario is, it was not unusual in our class. I knew exactly what was coming, well at least I thought I did, but on this day, she decided to take it to a whole new level. Every day she would humiliate a student in this way by having them bend over in front of the class and pretend to whack them on the butt. She made an entire show of it, and being the inclusive person she was, would involve the whole class in the show, including contorted facial expressions as she pretended to wind up the practice swings. The class obligingly joined in the laughter at her antics, somewhat reminiscent of Lord of the Flies, but mostly relieved that it wasn't them up there. In my case, instead of placing a book at the person's butt and whacking it so that it made a loud sound, she removed the book and hit me directly with the ruler. A wave of shock and humiliation went through me. And all this because I rounded up instead of down? This scenario started a fear in me that I continued to struggle with for a long time. My report card had the same comment for years after that, "Leanne has talent but lacks confidence". I wonder why? The irony was that God had called me to stand in front of crowds and deliver His message to them, yet this experience made me never want to be in front of a crowd... ever.

What experience in your life has birthed such fear? Fear is a crippling burden that speaks straight to the heart of not being enough. Because of fear we feel we aren't good enough to stand and speak to crowds; not smart enough to know who to trust and who to avoid. We feel we are unworthy of our God-given gifts and desires that will not only bring us fulfilment and joy, but also change the lives of others. How does fear affect your value and self-worth? Taking the time to discover your fears and how they impact you will enable you to free yourself from them and their effect on your self-worth.

Fear is a crippling burden that speaks straight to the heart of not feeling enough.

# Half Time Chat

The first half of this book has identified ways in which not being enough is communicated to us. We've talked about the times when people and situations have communicated to us that we are simply not enough. As we reach the halfway point and have a clearer idea of how we've been affected by not feeling enough, let's now start talking about ways of dealing with our feelings of unworthiness and moving forward in our lives. As I mentioned, there is not a one-time solution to this problem. I wish there was one thing we could do so that we never have to deal with feelings of unworthiness again. The reality is that we live in a fallen world and we ourselves are fallen people, so incidents are going to continually happen in our lives that will trigger feelings of unworthiness and not feeling enough. Counteracting those triggers is a lifelong journey. The good news is that there is a very simple, yet powerful way we can overcome those feelings and live our lives in freedom and truth. Let's face it, there are always going to be meanies, but if you implement what I am going to teach you, I guarantee you that in a very short time you'll notice that their words don't have the power they used to have. Just like Luke Skywalker in Return of the Jedi when the emperor's words lost their power to turn him to the dark side!

As you embrace the truths in these chapters you are going to feel the burden of unworthiness release off your life. It will be replaced by a peaceful assurance that is like an anchor steadying you when unworthiness knocks once again at your door. So, throw off all doubt and fear and let's get on with reclaiming our true value and worth.

Now is the time to grab your "I'm Enough Journal" and get to work. This journal is a great workbook for the remaining chapters to help navigate your feelings of unworthiness and reclaim your true value and worth.

If you have not got your "I'm Enough Journal" head to www.abidingprovidence.com/shop

I'm Enough

Chapter Seven

Survival

"When you know your value no one can make you feel worthless."

Edmund Hillary

Before Jesus performed a miracle, healed anyone or turned water into wine He first came to the edge of the river Jordan where John was baptising people and asked John to baptise Him. At first, John refused, insisting that it was he that needed baptising by Jesus rather than the other way around. But at Jesus' insistence John obeyed and Jesus went beneath the waters. As He came up the heavens opened and He saw the Spirit of God descending like a dove and settling on Him. A voice from heaven said, "This is my dearly loved Son, who brings Me great joy."

When we think about not being enough, we begin to understand the influence and impact it has on us. Such a powerful influence can only be overcome by something with greater power. The solution to not feeling enough is actually quite simple, but so hard to put into practice. The solution to releasing us from the trap of not feeling enough is right in front of us, yet we often struggle to embrace it. I suggest to you that the answer is in our Maker. Just as God spoke over Jesus as He was being baptised, declaring who He was and that God was well pleased with Him, God wants to speak words over us. He created an identity in us that He wants to see flourish and emerge. He has designed a purpose and direction for our lives, and God wants to see

The solution to not feeling enough is found in our Maker.

this fulfilled because He placed it inside us in the first place. It's so interesting that we marvel over the way God spoke to Jesus before Jesus even began to fulfil His calling. Up to then, Jesus hadn't performed any miracles, yet His Father found Him acceptable and loved Him, suggesting that our worth and value are not related to what we do, but rather to how our Father sees us.

It's true, our value and worth have absolutely nothing to do with how fast we can run, how tall we are, how much money we make or how popular or pretty we are. Our value and worth are not tied up in such frivolous things. The key to being free from feeling "not enough" is moving from trying to be accepted to knowing you are accepted by God. Our worth is innate, it has been birthed in us and given to us by God. We read in Genesis about Adam and Eve being the first of creation, created in the image of God. When we stop to take in that knowledge and think about the fact that we were created in the image of God, we can't help but know there is something worthwhile in us. There must be something of value, there must be something to hope for, given that we are created in His image. In Psalm 139, the Psalmist talks about how we were created by God. He said, "you made all the delicate inner parts of my body and knit me

The key to freedom from feeling "not enough" is moving away from trying to be accepted to knowing you are accepted by God.

together in my mother's womb". Thank you for making me so wonderfully complex. Your workmanship is marvellous. How well I know it. You watched me as I was being formed in utter seclusion and woven together in the darkness of the womb. You saw me. Before I was born, every day of my life was recorded in your book. Every moment was laid out before a single day passed." What a beautiful expression of our value in the sight of God, how even in the darkest places, where nobody else sees and nobody else knows, God is there. He creates and He marvels at His creation. In essence, He is showing off His creation in us.

I want to suggest to you that the key to negating unworthiness and feeling we are not enough comes down to seeing ourselves as God sees us. It's grabbing hold, with everything we have, of who we are and the truth of who God created us to be. When we do this we will no longer be deceived by the words of others and the pain of past incidents. Instead, we will walk with confidence in the truth of who God says we are.

I find it amazing that God still loves me in spite of everything I've done and all the times I've let Him down. I have wrestled with my relationship with God and not always seen eye to eye with Him. As I mentioned before, I can really relate to

We need to learn to see ourselves as God sees us.

the apostle Peter and his up-and-down relationship with Jesus. You might be able to relate to that as well and yet He still loves us unconditionally. Our struggle hasn't diminished His love or tarnished it in any way. His love remains strong and true. As we move away from the futile efforts of being accepted by others, and for some of us that also applies to pleasing God, we move towards the peace, security, confidence and freedom of actually knowing we are accepted. Jeremiah 29:11 reminds us that God has plans for us, plans for good and not disaster, and those plans give us hope and a future.

We have a future because of Him. Similarly, in Philippians 1:6 Paul says, "I am certain that God who began a good work in us will continue His work until it is finally finished on the day that Christ returns." We are a work in progress. Fighting against unworthiness and not feeling valuable is a process. It's something we will deal with off and on throughout our lives, and how well we deal with it and how we overcome it is directly related to how much we choose to understand and believe how God sees us and what He thinks of us. This is the key and the foundation for denying these feelings of unworthiness.

Proverbs 3 reminds us to trust in the Lord with all our heart and not depend on our own understanding. So often we substitute God's truth for our own understanding and experience, rather than laying that down and trusting in what He says. He goes on to say, "Seek His will in all you do, and He will make your paths straight". So, all this confusion and doubt and worry that we carry around will disappear and all will become clear when we focus on Him, trust in Him with all our heart and depend on Him and what He says, rather than the mess of our own understanding.

When Perfectionism becomes Poison

I am a self-confessed perfectionist. While this can be a wonderful quality for my employer or someone who has asked me to do something, it can be a real trap for me. How can something really be done perfectly in the first place? I used to lie awake for hours at night, beating myself up over what could have been done better and how I could have worked more efficiently.

A lot of us are plagued by perfectionism. Sometimes our upbringing has taught us that perfectionism is really important. Perhaps our parents had very high expectations that led us into a cycle of perfectionism. Perhaps we like the feeling of empowerment from getting everything right. Whatever started the cycle, continuing to seek perfection in order to validate our worth is a poisonous way to live. It means that every time we don't achieve perfection we confirm to ourselves that we are not enough. If we want to overcome feelings of unworthiness, we need to redefine perfection. When we think about how it plays out in our lives we begin to see what an impossible hill it is to climb. Take, for example, washing dishes. What's the perfect way to wash dishes? Is there even a perfect way to wash dishes? Is there a way it has to be done, and if it's not done that exact way is it not perfect?

Perfectionism should not be a yardstick for measuring our experiences in life. We need to be able to distinguish between perfectionism and doing something well or well enough, acknowledging that it may not be perfect but has been done to the best of our ability. Let me ask you a question. Who has the power to judge whether you are worthy or not? Who has the authority to do that? So often we give away our power to others and allow them to judge whether we are worthwhile or not. In Lauren Daigle's song, "You Say", she so beautifully describes God's view of us when we don't feel like we are worth much at all. She talks

If we want to overcome feelings of unworthiness, we need to redefine our definition of perfection.

about being loved when we don't feel it, strong when we feel weak and that we are His in the times that we feel we don't belong.

Sometimes we give that power away. It can be to the person on the street who abuses you in traffic, a teacher who doesn't like your work or a parent whose standards you can never meet. We give that power away to someone who couldn't possibly know our value and worth. The only one who can truly speak to our identity and worth is the one who created us... God.

I'm a survivor of relentless attacks on my identity, value and worth. Scattered throughout this book are stories that have communicated that I wasn't good enough, and the sad truth is there are many more. The reality is that I have survived those incidents and learned a lot. I'm sure that if we were to sit down over a cup of coffee you could break my heart with your own stories of how people communicated to you that you weren't enough. But guess what? You are also still standing. In spite of everything you've faced in your life, you are still standing. We are survivors.

When we take the time to press into God and hear what His plans and His heart are for us, we not only have that truth inside our head but also deep in our hearts. It transforms us and holds us steady, allowing us to continually get up when we are knocked down so that we are resilient in the face of not being good enough. It allows adversity to just fall off us like water off a duck's back.

In 2 Corinthians 12, Paul talks about taking pleasure in his weakness, in the insults and hardships, the persecutions and the troubles he suffered for Christ. He said, "When I am weak, then I am strong because it's God's strength that we lean on in those times, it's His power that gets us through". We need to know, understand and believe the truth, because we have a God who is miraculous. He's not a distant God, sitting up in heaven looking over us and waiting for us to mess up so He can punish us. He knows the hairs on our heads are all numbered and He knows the number, so there's no need for us to be afraid because we are valuable to God. More valuable than a whole flock of sparrows! When we allow that truth to penetrate our heart and mind it becomes a lighthouse that guides us and sets us apart. Knowing we are valuable to God breaks those crippling feelings of unworthiness. It's the only way to conquer them... God is the only way. This is the simple and profound message of this book. Other things in these pages will help you on your journey to freedom but they are only add-ons to this one truth. God is the only way and is the key. If you allow Him, He will reveal to you the wonder of your genesis and the glory of your future. He is the only way you will be able to walk in true unhindered freedom from feelings worthlessness.

Knowing we are valuable to God breaks those crippling feelings of unworthiness.

Now is the *Time* to overcome self doubt and reclaim your *Value* and worth.

Taking Action

1. Sit before God every day and ask how He sees you (this may take time, so be patient).

2. Write or describe what He showed you in a journal so you never forget it.

3. Look at it regularly throughout the day.

I'm Enough

Chapter Eight

Leaving Kids Behind

"Healing takes courage. We all have courage,
even if we have to dig a little to find it."

Tori Amos

I'm Enough

There's nothing like parenting to shine a light on feeling not enough. On any given day, there are countless opportunities to mess up. The scariest thing is that we're in charge of someone else's life, certainly in the early years. We have a huge influence on how they'll grow up, how they'll be moulded as productive human beings in society, not to mention their spiritual growth. There's just so much pressure! And then, of course, there are the other people out there that seem to be doing it so well. They parent with excellence while looking after their bodies, running successful businesses and cooking wholesome gourmet meals every night. And don't get me started on how environmentally friendly they are!

There are so many opportunities to feel like a failure as parents. But as my kids have reached their late teens and young adulthood, I've actually stopped to admire the really great people they've become. They've survived all my parenting failures, including what might be called the "forgotten" series. One of these involved leaving one of the kids in the car while I took the others into school. Another resulted in our pastor calling to see if I'd accidentally left anything at church, which turned out to be one of our kids. Then there was the time I was so engrossed in a conversation with one child in the car that I left the other at the shops, only realising my mistake when a driver signalled that my kid was chasing the car down the street! Nothing that a few counselling sessions on abandonment won't fix! In spite of all this, my kids are giving and loving, committed and respectful, most of the time. And I like to think I've contributed to that.

And yes, there have been times that I've not felt good enough as a mum, for not driving my kids all over town seven days a week for their sport or their dancing. Or not as good as the mum who's able to do their maths homework with them. By the way, when my boys started doing long division at school, I thought to myself, "I'm going to learn how to do this with them. I'm going to finally grasp how to do long division." Remember the rounding incident with Mrs Allen? Well, it turns out I suck at long division as well. Both my boys learned it and moved on without me getting it at all. Then my girls got to learning long division and I thought, "I'm going to nail it now. I'm older and so much wiser and I'm going to master my evil nemesis." But again, I missed it. I do not get long division, I just don't. So I've decided I don't need long division in my life and am so thankful to God for creating calculators so that I don't have to worry about long division anymore. I'm going to give Him a big high five when I get to heaven. The reality is that the only maths I've ever needed to know was percentages, "Excuse me sales assistant, is that dress 20% off or 50%?" Can I hear an amen! I've just had to let go of ever learning long division and feel freer because of it. So, in spite of all my failings, my kids have turned out great. They're happy, they're secure, they know God and they're getting on with their lives.

Sometimes we feel like the past hurts, particularly the childhood experiences, have set us up for failure. The pain is so deeply ingrained in us that we feel like we're never ever going to get over it. But I want to assure you that change and breakthrough is possible because Christ makes all things possible. It is possible for even the deepest wounds to be healed, for us to rebuild from our experiences and not have to walk with a limp. Isaiah 53 says, "He was pierced for our rebellion, crushed for our sins. He was beaten so that we could become whole. He was whipped so that we could be healed." Jesus went through what He did on the cross to give us an opportunity to live our lives in the knowledge that we are enough. We are so highly prized by God that He sent His Son to pay the price for our sins, so that we can be whole because of Him.

We are so highly prized by God that He sent His Son to pay the price for our sins, so that we can become whole because of Him.

I'm Enough

The message of the cross communicates the truth that we are worthy, not because of anything we've done, but because of Christ's sacrifice for us. Psalm 34 says, "The Lord hears His people when they call to Him for help. He rescues them from all their troubles. He's close to the broken-hearted. He rescues those whose spirits are crushed. The righteous person faces many troubles, but the Lord comes to rescue each time, for the Lord protects the bones of the righteous, not one of them is broken." That's incredible. What an amazing promise that is, to know that He's close to the broken-hearted. How often do we feel broken-hearted alone and wonder why we're just not enough? Our hearts hurt when we feel unworthy. Our spirits are crushed by relentless feelings of not being enough, and every time we get up it seems like we get knocked down again. But the remarkable truth is that the Lord is there to rescue us every time. When we call to Him for help, He is more than able to heal us from past hurts and set us free. Jesus said, "Come to me, all of you who are weary and heavy with burdens, and I'll give you rest. Take my yoke upon you, let me teach you because I'm humble and gentle of heart and you will find rest for your souls. My yoke is easy to bear and the burden I give you is light." Wow! What an opportunity it is to lay down those burdens of pain and have Him teach us how to navigate them because He's humble and gentle of heart. Some of us have had harsh teachers in life, the meanies as I like to call them, who have taught us things in very scary and painful ways, but Jesus is gentle and humble of heart and that's how He teaches us. With gentleness and humility, He's going to bring us through and heal us from past hurts.

Speaking of moving forward, I've asked myself whether or not I've grown in this area of not feeling enough, and I can see some significant changes in my life that let me know I've made progress. I remember as a teenager I used to dress quite provocatively to get male attention. As previously mentioned, my father left when I was very young, so there was a lack of positive male influence in my life. Inside me there was a little girl hungering for a father's attention. So how does a girl in her teenage years get male attention? Usually by dressing and behaving provocatively. I remember wanting that attention, but when I reflect on it now, that need has gone completely and I no longer look for male attention. I like my husband's attention, but he's the only male whose attention I'm interested in. Everything changed for me when I discovered my identity in Christ, and the revelation of God's overwhelming love and acceptance healed the wounds left by abandonment. He filled the hunger for male attention with His love and I learned who He says I am. And because I now know the truth, there's no need for that affirmation and attention from other males. He's my Father, He speaks to that and uses my husband to speak to that too. And through that healing of childhood hurt I've become completely free. It's the same for any childhood hurt that you are trying to fill on your own. I like to call them God-shaped holes: Holes in our heart that we are desperately trying to fill with things like shopping, alcohol, drugs, relationships and any number of other things. The reality is that those things cannot fill a God-shaped hole, only He can. We can drive ourselves crazy and wear other people out by trying to fill holes that only God can minister to. When we allow God to heal us, we no longer have to manage our pain and we get to enjoy the freedom of being released.

Being Dumb

Psychologists use a term called self-compassion and define it as one of the keys to overcoming feelings of unworthiness. Self-compassion is learning how to love and care for yourself. How kind are you to yourself? Being kind to yourself may sound like a simple thing, but the reality is that many of us struggle to do it, especially those of us who continually strive for perfection. Have you ever had someone say something nice to you and inside your head your thoughts are screaming that they have it wrong and you don't deserve the compliment? Or maybe you hear how God loves you and despite rationalising it in your mind your heart is having trouble receiving it? How many of us know that hearing it and actually receiving it deep inside our hearts are two completely different things? When we struggle to receive that love from God, we will often struggle to receive love from others.

When we're in pain we often reject people. We do it to protect ourselves from bringing people close for fear they may hurt us even more. I've done that so many times. But to have self-compassion and to let ourselves off the hook helps us navigate through those times by reinforcing the truth of who we are. I don't know about you, but I'm probably my own worst critic and have berated and torn myself apart over my mistakes in life. I've gone well beyond the cruel words of others. I remember being told that I was dumb as a kid, and even though this only happened once or twice, it was enough to make it stick. And ever since then, I've repeated those very same words in my heart again and again and again, "You're just dumb." How about you? How hard are you on yourself?

The funny thing about life is that situations will come along that seem to confirm those thoughts and you'll go, "Yes, see that's right, I am dumb." It might be something as simple as a quiz night and answering a question wrong and inside you think, "Yeah, that's right. I'm dumb." Life has a way of confirming things that we fear the most. Going to Bible college was incredibly challenging for me because I thought, "I'm too dumb to go to Bible college. I just can't, I just can't do it. It's just not possible." And then I thought, "No, I really feel God is saying for me to go." And so I went and told myself, "I'm not just going to go. I'm actually going to pass the course with distinction."

Like El in Legally Blonde, I confronted something that I thought I'd never be able to do and achieved my goal of passing with distinction. Except, I didn't wear pink and have a dog named Bruiser!

It's good to question and push ourselves beyond the tapes playing inside our heads. When we say to ourselves, "I'm not good enough" it's wise to ask, "Is that true?" It's so important for us to stop and fact check the words that we're speaking to ourselves. Psalm 103 reminds us, "All that I am, praise the Lord, may I never forget the good things that He's done for me, He forgives all my sins and He heals all my diseases, He redeems me from death and crowns me with love and tender mercies." In His eyes, we are crowned with His tender mercies. That's how valuable and important we are to God. We've been adopted into His family as children of the living God, so much so that He sent His Son to make that possible. The solution to not feeling enough is found in us and our choice to trust in God's love. The solution begins by calling out to Him and sharing with Him the painful things of our past. It involves uncensored and genuine sharing of how we feel and what we think of those involved. Only then will we be ready for God to begin the healing process, starting with asking

God to speak into that painful situation and sharing His truth. I have found that gaining this understanding from Him allowed me to release those painful situations to Him and receive His healing. It can be a slow process, and a painful one, but it's well worth the time and effort. When we are able to gain His perspective and truth on how He sees us it frees us to move forward with our lives. Healing from past hurts allows us to receive love, especially God's love, without the need for self-protection and fear.

The solution to not feeling enough is found in our decision to trust in God's love.

Now is the *Time* to overcome self doubt and reclaim your *Value* and worth.

Taking Action

1. Ask God to show you a time in your past when you felt not enough.

2. Ask Him to show you where He was when that was happening.

3. Then ask God to show you His truth and how He sees you.

I'm Enough

Chapter Nine

Ready, Steady, Go!

"Comparison is a thief of all joy."

Theodore Roosevelt

I'm Enough

When David showed up on the battlefield, he wasn't prepared for what God was calling him to do. He had no armour and no swords. All he had was a slingshot. As we know, he was there to feed his brothers and check up on them, yet he suddenly found himself the only one with enough courage, or arrogance according to his brothers, to go up against Goliath. Saul agreed to this crazy plan and gave David his armour for protection. Considering this young boy was about to go and fight a battle-hardened giant, supplying him with armour was the least he could do. I wonder if they thought, "we need to give this poor kid some protection, to give him at least a sporting chance of not being killed by the first blow?" However, David found that the armour didn't fit. It was heavy, the wrong shape for his body and he wasn't used to wearing it. When David fought bears and lions he never wore any armour, so it just didn't feel right. Everyone saw David as a scrawny little kid and decided he needed to wear what everyone else was wearing in order to be successful. They also ignored the fact that the ones who were wearing armour were hiding in their tents! David took off the armour and went into battle against Goliath in the only way he knew how: armed with his slingshot, stones and God on his side.

As we fight this battle against not feeling enough, we learn to run our race as David did. Saul wanted to put his armour on David so that David did it his way, but God wanted David to go about things in his own authentic way. God knew David had conviction and from an early age had ran his own race with God and achieved victory.

As we discussed in chapter 5, comparisons are so defeating. Running our own race is liberating because there's nothing to compare with and therefore nothing to put ourselves down about. Our race is individual and unique. Even if I don't run my race perfectly, who's to say that everything is ruined? Perhaps God has asked me to do something and I haven't done it straight away. Perhaps I have to go around the block a couple of times before I decide to be obedient. All is not lost. Jonah is a great example of this. He didn't want to give God's message to the meanies, so he ran away and became the first human sushi, a raw man eaten by a fish (thanks to Levi Lusko for this one). Jonah then decided to do what he was told and all the meanies were transformed and saved. In the same way, I can pick myself up and continue on after failing to do what God asks me to do. God doesn't give up on me and God doesn't give up on you. The important thing is to continue running our own race before us, not someone else's.

Fisherman

In Exodus 20, one of the instructions given to the Israelites is not to covet your neighbour's house. It states, "You must not covet your neighbour's wife, male or female servant, ox or donkey or anything that belongs to a neighbour", because it's in wanting what someone else has that we run into trouble. We struggle for no good reason because we have veered off track into someone else's journey and were never supposed to be there in the first place. It's so tempting to look at other people's lives and want what they have, but in wanting what they have we miss the great opportunities that God has for us. Corinthians 2 reminds us, "Don't worry about the other men around you that tell you how important they are." There are people out there who are more than happy to tell you how fabulous their life is and there really isn't anything wrong with that. We are supposed to rejoice and be happy for one another, but how many times do we find our faces etched with a frozen smile as they tell us how good they are and how full of adventure and excitement their lives are. And behind our smiles our worth is eroding away inside because our own journey seems to be a dud in comparison to theirs.

We feel like we've missed out and we should be doing more. And dare I say it, we feel not enough.

Once I went to a gathering designed to encourage and inspire women which included a panel of women sharing their experiences. As they went around the circle my ability to connect with them dwindled as they shared their resumes of amazing life opportunities brimming with accolades. I heard about doctorates and double degrees while running their own successful businesses, and in their spare time (apparently, they had some) they'd written five best sellers! After the first double degree intimidation started to set in and I began to feel pathetic as if I was living in a completely different universe. I understood the purpose of talking about their credentials to verify their authority to speak on the topic, but when I heard double degrees and doctorates I immediately thought, "Oh, I'm not even in the same realm as this person, how can I possibly relate to them?"

Interestingly, when I reflect on that situation and Jesus' methods for choosing valuable voices, He didn't say, "I'm looking for double-degreed people to influence the world" or "I'm looking for people who've written the five best selling books." He entrusted God's lifesaving message of redemption, one of the most significant messages ever heard, to mostly uneducated fishermen. Consider that for a while. An uneducated, rough-and-ready bunch of larrikins received the ultimate privilege of being the first to share the gospel message! Don't ever think that without a list of accolades your life is not valuable and worthwhile. Jesus chose fishermen and He chose you too. You have something unique and powerful to offer to the world.

Let me just clarify that I've got nothing against doctorates or study. I absolutely love study and admire people who have gone to such lengths to become so proficient. What I'm saying is that when it comes to our journeys, it is unique and equally valid for everyone, doctorate or not. Don't allow comparisons to take you out of the race and make you feel like you're not enough. Taking a different path doesn't mean that we're less or not enough, because God uses all kinds of people in all kinds of situations. So, I always remember the fishermen. We can take that thought one step further. Throughout Scripture Jesus also spoke to children, widows and lepers. He ate with tax collectors and chose women as the first to witness His resurrection. God is not looking at our accolades, He's looking for willing hearts.

God is not looking at our accolades, He's looking for willing hearts.

I'm Enough

As we choose to face our feelings of unworthiness, it's important to focus on what God has designed for us, rather than what He is doing for others. Comparing ourselves to others invites the spirit of intimidation in. We feel small and incapable compared to others, but the reality is there is always someone further down the track. No one can be the best at everything, so instead of allowing intimidation to paralyse, you can use it to see what is possible. After all, the same blood runs through all of us. I used to sit in church and see great speakers take to the platform. I longed to be up there, sharing the message God had put in my heart. As others received favour and opportunities I felt more and more defeated, until I learned about running my own race. When I learned to keep my eyes focused on what was in front of me those feelings of insecurity disappeared. There are times when they rise up again, but I am so much more aware that I'm drifting into someone else's lane and need to get back into mine.

Team Player

In 2022 Ash Barty, our famous Australian tennis player was ranked the number one women's tennis player in the world. In interviews, she consistently referred to her team and even though we only see her on court, she is in fact part of a team. Wouldn't it be great to have a team: a whole group of people dedicated to every aspect of our lives, helping us to get the best out of it? She has a coach who trains her, dieticians who guide what she eats, trainers and physio s who keep her body functioning... the list goes on and on. All these people are alongside her with one common goal: to help her succeed by playing to the best of her ability. Imagine all that wisdom and experience going into every aspect of your life? John 14:16-17 says, "I will ask the Father and He will send you a helper, who will never leave you. He is the Holy Spirit who leads in all truth." In God's grace and mercy He has sent us a helper who is better than any team we could ever put together. If we allow Him the Holy Spirit will guide us in every area of our lives, prompting us when we need to rest, making us aware of things to come, warning us about poor decisions and confirming that our footsteps are going in the right direction. He is on our team all the time, equipping us with everything we need to run the race before us. We only need to decide if we are going to partner with Him. What would happen to Ash Barty if she decided to ignore her team or only listened to them once a month? What would her progress look like? What if she decided to follow another player's strategy and ignored the advice and wisdom of those who know her and know how to get the best out of her. It would end in disaster. Her performance would drop and she would struggle.

We do this all the time with the Holy Spirit by ignoring His promptings, going our own way and choosing to follow the advice of others rather than listening to His voice. While it would be great to have a team, the Holy Spirit is so much better. It's just different from what we expect and requires a little more effort to seek and listen. How much help we receive is determined purely by us and our willingness to follow Him. We have a helper who is with us all the time. He never takes holidays or sick days and promises to be with us forever. He is willing and able to help us run our own race to the best of our ability with the skills and talent that God has given us, so that we can succeed.

One of the best ways to be successful in running our own race is to stop comparing ourselves with others, and instead, measure our success and progress against our own achievements. If I want to improve my health I could measure my general health and start making changes to my eating, exercise and rest. I could then re-evaluate those measurements in three months. Choosing to compare myself to Mary, who has a different body shape, a different time schedule and a metabolism that's off the Richter scale is not only ridiculous but an utter waste of time. It's not going to work and it's just going to be self-defeating. But when I see progress in myself, I can truly rejoice and enjoy the benefits and rewards of my success, because it's a true reflection of my growth and a sign that I am moving away from not feeling enough.

It is possible to overcome feelings of unworthiness and not being enough, and a big step towards this is learning to run our own race. Did you know that when horses race they have blinkers on their eyes to block out their peripheral vision? This gives them a clear vision of the lane in front of them. It blocks out the other horses so they remain totally focused on their own race. We need to do that too when it comes to the path that God has carved out before us, because the minute we start looking in someone else's lane we end up off track, and that's when life gets rocky and unsettled. When we run our own race we can look at someone else who's achieving more success and rather than being intimidated, cheer them on. We can say, "Well done. That's her timing. God's got me on my own journey." It allows us to encourage the person who has a wonderful marriage when yours is challenging and not really working. Running our own race gives us the confidence in knowing that there's a timing for all things. God wants us to pray into situations for our own journey. It may be that someone else's career is taking off and they are getting opportunity after opportunity, and you wonder, "Why aren't I getting that?" What God is saying is, "I want you to run your race. My timing is perfect, and my ways are good and when you stay on track with your blinkers on and follow the path that I have laid out before you, you will also have success."

We need to learn to

run our own race.

Now is the *Time* to overcome self doubt and reclaim your *Value* and worth.

Taking Action

1. Ask God to show you the areas in your life where you have been running someone else's race.

2. Ask God for forgiveness for those areas and ask him to show you why you felt the need to do that?

3. Ask God to give you a fresh revelation of the race He has set before you.

I'm Enough

Chapter Ten

Hearing Voices

"Do not allow negative thoughts to enter your mind for they are weeds that strangle confidence."

Bruce Lee

I'm Enough

As I mentioned previously, I was in my 20s when I was hit by depression. I say "hit" because it came out of nowhere and completely struck me down. I'd never experienced anything like it before, a dark cloud that unexpectedly showed up and took up residence over my head, completely zapping me of all joy and happiness. During this time I became aware of the voices in my head, the voices that no one else hears and knows about and can have a very powerful influence on our lives. Because no one else hears our voices, we can get away with being the biggest meanies to ourselves. I call it a silent epidemic, because no one can call us out and say, "Hey, that's ridiculous, cut it out". If we're not aware of what we're saying to ourselves, negative self-talk can become one of our biggest saboteurs.

When I think of negative thoughts that torment and sabotage our lives I remember King Saul. Saul had been chosen by God to rule his people after they insisted on having a king, but it wasn't long before the power went to Saul's head and due to his disobedience God took away His favour. Along with this punishment came a tormenting spirit. Saul struggled with this spirit and only found peace when David, a man after God's heart played the harp for him.

There have been times in my life when the thoughts raging around in my mind have been overwhelming. They felt like what I imagine Saul's torment must have been like and I followed his example and listened to worship music. It's incredible how quickly that torment disappears when one is worshipping God. I can move from a state of chaos and anxiety to a peace that transcends all understanding. There is power and peace in declaring out loud who God is. Just the mere mention of His name is enough to calm the raging seas, and it not only happens with worship it also happens with God's word. What I learned from my first experience of depression was the power of the mind and the power of Scripture to change the mind. Negative voices can be extinguished with Scripture and with methodical precision negative thoughts can be replaced with ones that breathe life back into you. These negative voices are a silent epidemic and it's up to us to be aware of them, measure them against God's truth and do something about it, otherwise we will carry them around for years, while feelings of not being enough will continue to haunt us. What's more, they will grow and overcome us.

Studies have shown that we think much faster than we speak. We speak approximately 125 words per minute, but think around 12,000 to 14,000 words per minute. I remember when I started producing one minute segments for radio. This was a challenge as I have a lot of thoughts to pack into that short space! So instead of simplifying my script I just said it faster. I know the theory is flawed, but it served me well for a little while. After getting feedback that it was hard to keep up with me I learned to choose my words more carefully and slow down the pace. Knowing that our thought life is so active means that words have a huge influence on how we see things around us. Fourteen thousand words are a lot! And if they're primarily negative, it's no wonder we struggle with our self worth. The scary truth is that if we choose to entertain a particular thought for an extended period of time, that thought eventually becomes automatic, which means we don't even realise we're thinking it. How sobering is that? When the thought is negative or based on lie it can become part of us without us realising it. It can also become detrimental when we sabotage ourselves by accepting it as truth.

It's critical that we are attentive and realise the nature of the words that we speak to ourselves. To do this takes a lot of courage. God hasn't given us a spirit of fear and timidity, but one of power, love and self-discipline. It's because of the Holy Spirit that we can attack and extinguish these negative thought patterns when they invade our lives. It takes discipline to call ourselves out when we fall into the trap of negative self-talk because it's much easier to let it continue, especially if we're used to doing it. Negative self-talk keeps us in a state of self-loathing and doesn't require us to expect more of ourselves, and even though something is not working for us, we sometimes continue doing it because it's easier than making the effort to change. This is why we need to call on the Holy Spirit, to stop us from settling for what is easy and familiar and press on with something different that will impact us in positive ways.

Philippians 4 talks about not worrying about anything and praying about everything. Prayer is so critical. We should never underestimate the power of prayer to change a situation. Prayer is where we are set free from these negative mindsets and know the truth. Peace can come from having conversations with God and allowing Him to speak to us, even during difficult times. Scripture teaches us that the peace He gives will guard our hearts and minds in Christ Jesus. This is really important because, "Out of the heart is the wellspring of life." When we trust God to transform the way we think we break those patterns of not feeling enough. By allowing Him to speak into the thoughts that we've had for years we replace negative thoughts with the truth, without realising it. When we allow the Holy Spirit to sift through those thoughts, He brings His truth to counter the lies we've believed for so long. It's so beautiful that the Holy Spirit helps us in our weakness. He knows our deepest struggles and wants to help us. Sometimes I don't know what to pray and I don't know what to do. I feel conflicted and don't know what the truth is in my life. This is when I lean heavily on the Holy Spirit to reveal the truth, to clarify and unravel what has been knotted up for so long and to bring truth and life to it.

In his book "I Declare War", Levi Lusko wrote about naming the negative voice in our head. He suggested this so that we become more aware of that voice and

When we allow the Holy Spirit to sift our thoughts, He brings His truth to oppose the lies we've believed for so long.

what it's saying. He even had a name for his negative voice, calling him "Evil Levi." Psychologists and mentors agree there is something about naming and identifying negative thoughts that empowers us to question their validity and tackle them head on. In this way we become more proficient at recognising the voice when it arises and countering its attack. You may have more than a few negative words going on in your head: it could be a whole story. There have been times in my life when I've created a whole story about what's going on from a mere few facts. The problem is that I don't know what's going on in other people's minds. Wouldn't that be a great superpower to have? To be able to read people's minds and know what they're thinking? Just like Xavier in X-men I would never be in any doubt about what others were thinking. Mmmm, on second thoughts, maybe I don't want to know. Mind control sounds better, "This is not the droid you are looking for!"

When we choose to entertain the story in our head it has a significant impact on the decisions we make. If we believe certain things about a situation, regardless of whether it's true or not, it will affect how we respond.

The solution to the battlefield in our mind starts with identifying the story in our head and questioning it.

I'm Enough

The solution to the battlefield in our mind starts with identifying the story that's going on inside our heads and asking ourselves important questions like, "Is this story true? Is how I'm perceiving the situation actually true?" When it comes to our relationships with other people and what we perceive they are thinking, it's important to ask ourselves if it's actually true? Do I know for a fact that's what they are thinking?" Or is there another possibility? If we can rationalise our thoughts it lifts a huge weight of mental anguish off our shoulders.

I have a confession to make. I'm a big self-talker and talk to myself all the time. People must think I'm crazy. My kids sometimes ask, "Who are you talking to?" In my defence, I talk because I'm very analytical and it's how I process things. I have great conversations with myself. The good news is I haven't answered myself back yet, so I don't have to be shipped off to the funny farm just yet! In all seriousness there is something really positive in being able to talk to yourself and bring thoughts up into your conscious mind for interrogation. Psychologists say it's a useful way of identifying and critiquing our thoughts. I've also heard that athletes use self-talk in preparation for sport, and I reckon if athletes can talk to themselves then I can too! They do this to motivate themselves and prepare for a race, talk about how they're feeling, what they're going to do in the race and the outcome they want. So with the power vested in me I give you permission today to speak to yourself because it can be a powerful way of unlocking negative thoughts that fly under the radar and insidiously invade our lives. Another powerful strategy is to write down what you're thinking. Seeing your thoughts written down in black and white can be quite shocking and is another powerful way of checking just how pervasive negative thoughts can be. Many people have discovered the power of journaling to clarify and correct their thought lives.

Winning Relationships

Even though our inner thoughts are concealed from the outside world they have a way of manifesting in our behaviour. Take for example a situation where you're meeting people for the first time and you're feeling anxious about it. You might say to yourself, "These people are not going to like me, I'm not funny, popular, intelligent or interesting enough for them to like me." This type of thought pattern often becomes a reality because we behave out of our thoughts. If we believe that people are not going to like us, certain behaviours and impressions that we subconsciously exhibit actually repel them. In essence, our thoughts become self-fulfilling prophecies that confirm what's already inside our head, "See, I knew they wouldn't like me."

On the flip side, rather than wanting to win people over, our goal should simply be to connect with people. If our goal is to connect with others, it doesn't matter that we have different thoughts and opinions from them. We may be totally different and may not ever see each other again. We are merely connecting to get to know someone in the moment. Bringing a different attitude to a situation brings about positive outcomes. It is so critical that we harness the voice in our head and become aware of it. When we do that, we're able to reduce the power and authority of those words in determining our choices. Healthy life-giving thoughts are aligned with the word of God and what He says about us, and when we allow His word to have priority, His truth will reign supreme in our lives.

Rather than wanting to win people over, our goal should simply be to connect with people.

In Romans 15 Paul says, "I pray that God, the source of hope will fill you completely with joy and peace because you trust in Him." As we trust in Him, He fills us with joy and peace and, "then you will overflow with confident hope through the power of the Holy Spirit." By trusting in Him and allowing the Holy Spirit to work in our lives we can deal with these negative voices and be set free from them.

When we allow His Word to have priority, His truth will reign supreme in our lives.

I'm Enough

Now is the *Time* to overcome self doubt and reclaim your *Value* and worth.

Taking Action

1. Start to become aware of the thoughts you have during the day. You may like to write them down.

2. Are the majority of the words negative or positive?

3. Are they truthful or lies?

4. Bring the words you speak over yourself to God and ask Him to shed His light on them.

I'm Enough

Chapter Eleven

Sticks and Stones

"If you don't set a baseline standard for what you will accept in life, you'll find it easy to slip into behaviors and attitudes or a quality of life that is far below what you deserve."

Tony Robbins

My brother and I went to my dad's house to see him almost every weekend. Some years later my dad met someone and they started living together. This person already had children from previous marriages. There was instant competition. Every weekend we would arrive at a house that wasn't ours, with nothing in it of ours. We felt like visitors to a family that wasn't our own. The day Dad announced they were getting married I was fine about it. I was pretty young and didn't understand all the implications. It was just the way life went, and I was used to going with the flow, because what can you do anyway to change things? When you're so little, you don't really have a voice. What really hurt me was being told by one of the kids that "When your dad marries my mum, he's going to be my dad, not yours anymore." The words hung in the air with heaviness and finality. As a little kid, hearing that was gut-wrenching, having already felt I'd lost my dad when he left. I was hanging on by a thread to my relationship with him and now to hear he was not going to be my dad anymore was painful. The pain of the loss was deep and lonely.

Here's my point, life will throw a whole heap of scenarios at us and some of those are cruel. I know some of you have stories to tell that are far more gut-wrenching than mine. Unfortunate and painful things happen in our lives and all these incidents strongly communicate that we are not worthy or worthwhile, that we're not enough and that we need to do or be something more. Knowing your worth and value in Christ is the absolute key to breaking free from a world of "I'm not enough", so that when someone says to you that your dad's not your dad anymore or your parents disown you because of a decision you've made, you can stand firm and strong because your value is not anchored in their opinion of you. You then become impervious to a world that speaks these things over you and makes you jump over all these hurdles to be accepted and valued and worthwhile. Let's revisit Christ's baptism. Christ emerged from the waters of baptism and the heavens opened and God spoke. He declared who Jesus was for all to hear, clearly stating that Jesus was His Son and He was pleased with Him. Fast forward 40 days and what was the first question Satan asked as he attempted to deceive Jesus? "If you are the Son of God turn these stones into bread". Right off the bat, Satan attempted to challenge Jesus even though he had been validated by God Himself. If Jesus came up against this type of absurd questioning, why are we surprised when it happens to us? Our identity is often the first thing Satan questions because when we step off God's firm foundation we experience life on shaky ground.

Knowing our God-given value simplifies things because God is the only One we are turning to for our value and worth. God is our creator and therefore He has the credentials. Genesis 1:27 says, "God created human beings in His own image." We have all been created in the image of God. That's an incredible thought. He thought of us and had the desire to create human beings that reflect Him, with His characteristics and similarities. How incredible is that? But it doesn't stop there. We read that He adopted us in advance, so before we even accepted He'd decided to adopt us into His family. We're adopted. We're not alone. We are accepted by Him. Even with our insecurities and our shortcomings, we are accepted by God. He sent His Son to die for us so that we would be joined with Him in unconditional love. Unconditional love is a deep and intimate connection that does not require us to behave in a strict or impossible way to please Him. He has joined us to Him through His Son and His sacrifice and we're no longer slaves to sin. He's freed us from that and we are no longer slaves (Galatians 4:7). On this earth we are known as His body, fulfilling His purposes and plans. I love the way 1 Peter 2:9 says, "You are a chosen people, a royal priesthood, a holy nation, God's very own possession." Originally that was a reference to the Israelites, but we are now part of that

God is our Creator and therefore He has the credentials to speak in to our identity and worth.

family line because of Christ. We have been grafted into that line and its now part of our identity, so we can claim it too.

I'm sure you've had something that you loved, a possession, something that you owned that was very special to you. I had a toy dog called Bones and I remember we bought him from Coles. We were buying one as a gift for our babysitter and I loved dogs so my mum bought me one as well. Bones became my lifelong companion, to the point that when I was first married I hid him under the bed and still slept with him under my arm. It took a while to get used to not sleeping with him, because I'd pretty much slept with him from the age of about five. Bones was unbelievably ugly, tattered and dirty. He was brown, which was a good thing. But I loved him. He was my prize possession. I remember many hospital stays, caused by my brother, where my parents had to go to the house and bring Bones back to the hospital because I wouldn't sleep without him. You may be thinking about your prized possession, something that you couldn't do without and you just loved. And even though it looked mangy and was of no worth to anyone else, you saw the value in it and you absolutely loved it. Well, God sees us the same way when He says that we are His prized possessions. Even though we're a little roughed up, a little old, a little battle-weary, we are still

His prized possessions. That's an incredible thought to dwell on. You are God's prized possession, and because of that we're His children. He's our Father. We can call Him Father, Abba Father. And we can have that childlike relationship with Him. We can find that security, love and tenderness in Him that we would like to receive from a parent.

It's so important for us to know our value and worth in Christ. It's the key to breaking free from feelings of not being good enough and we have to keep reminding ourselves. That's why it's so important for us to stay in Scripture and not just gloss over the verses that talk about us no longer being slaves and being children of the Most High God. We are His masterpiece and His own possession. These verses drive home the message that we have been grafted into His family line and adopted by God, and they speak to our value and worth. When that drops from our heads into our hearts we can operate out of that reality on a regular basis. And when the hurtful words come, and they will, they will be like arrows that bounce off the armour and fall to the floor. They will not penetrate our hearts and cause damage and strife. When we take these values on board, change starts to happen. We walk a little taller. We feel more confident and we see the world in a different light. As we develop our sense of self-worth, we operate out of our values rather than our feelings. It is dangerous to rely on feelings to make wise decisions because they are so subjective and can vary on any given day, but the values that we hold dear and true in our lives are like anchors that steady us and allow us to be our authentic selves.

As we develop our sense of self-worth, we operate out of our values rather than our feelings.

Now is the *Time* to overcome self doubt and reclaim your *Value* and worth.

Taking Action

1. Take some time to list the Scriptures that talk about who God says you are.

2. Now ask God to speak to you personally about who He says you are. God is not a copy-and-paste kind of God, so while there are some universal things about us, there are also some unique things that He wants you to know.

3. Place these verses on your bathroom mirror or in your journal where you will see them often.

4. Memorise at least one of these verses so you can take it with you wherever you go.

5. Begin to journal the worthwhile and valuable things that you do every day for yourself, your family and your community.

I'm Enough

Chapter Twelve

Planning for the Future

> "You gain strength, courage and confidence by every experience in which you really stopped to look fear in the face. You were able to say to yourself, I lived through this horror. I can take the next thing that comes along."
>
> **Eleanor Roosevelt**

I love this quote from Eleanor Roosevelt because I've faced many fears in my life and survived. I may be a little weary and somewhat worse for wear, but at the end of the day they didn't kill me, I survived and I'm still putting one foot in front of the other. And so are you.

As we fight this battle of not feeling good enough, we too can have victories, survive and move forward to great things. One of the ways that moves us forward and frees us from staying trapped in this perpetual cycle of unworthiness is having plans. We talk about God's purposes and plans so He is an integral part of defining and designing our plans. When we engage in those plans we see transformation in our lives.

I'd never heard of a life plan until a couple of years ago. When I was introduced to it I found it life-changing. I'm an organiser and planner by nature and I understand this may be a struggle for people who like to live more spontaneously, but I have found the benefits life-changing. I enjoy thinking about the areas of my life that are important, bringing them before God and asking Him to reveal to me what His plans are. Things like my marriage, my relationship with God, my ministry, my relationship with my kids, my own health and wellbeing. I've had only positive results from thinking about these things, asking God to give me a picture of what He wants them to look like, and then measuring that against reality and working on the difference.

There's power in setting goals and cultivating healthy habits in our lives. I read a fantastic book called Atomic Habits, in which James Clear talks about getting rid of our bad habits and picking up good ones. It may seem easy at first, but forming good habits and setting goals to constantly move forward can be quite challenging, because life happens, doesn't it? I mean, if you've ever set yourself a goal of exercising, an aberration to most of us, something inevitably derails you. You may get a cold or the kids get sick and your routine gets mucked up. Before you know it two months have passed and you haven't done a thing. Or you may be starting something new and you're waiting for the sweet spot that happens at around 12 weeks, but in the meantime it really hurts and you're forcing yourself to do it until it becomes more of a habit. They say it used to take 30 days to form a habit, but now it's taking more like 90 days. It takes a while to get into a pattern where something becomes ingrained in our routine. When we're struggling with not feeling enough, it's so important to think about goals and the habits we want to nurture. It could be that focusing on the wrong things is the reason why we're not feeling enough. Perhaps we're

There's power in setting goals and cultivating healthy habits in our lives.

comparing ourselves with someone else or trying to live up to the expectations of others. We may even find that the things we're striving for aren't actually what we want in the first place because they don't make us happy. Maybe they don't bring life and love into our lives and they're demoralising. Looking at our goals and assessing how we're living our lives can address these things and change them.

I love the fact that we can change things for the better and we can do this starting today. It may only be one little thing and doesn't have to be an entire overhaul of your life that causes your spouse to say, "Who are you? When I left for work this morning you were this way and now I've come back and you're completely different." It could just be one little thing that makes all the difference so it's important to tap into what we were created to do – it's where the excitement and fullness of life comes.

Earlier, I mentioned that I did a leadership strengths test. I'm not a big fan of tests because I'm always the one that doesn't get a clear result. I'm kind of in the middle and often find the information doesn't help me. So I was a bit apprehensive about the strengths in leadership test but I'd heard good things about it and thought the results would be helpful. After answering all the questions, you're provided with a profile of your top five leadership strengths. I found it empowered me so much because there are so many variations. There are around 34 different strengths, so it's not a cookie-cutter process and mine will be very different from yours. The test confirmed things that I've felt in my heart for a long time, so it sat well with me. You know that feeling when a goal that you're really excited about or something that you've been working towards fills you with so much energy and excitement? That's what I felt.

Interestingly, the thing that people had criticised me about in the past actually turned out to be one of my strengths. So, it was very empowering. It's important for us to know where our strengths lie. We're not good at everything, we can't be superwoman, she doesn't actually exist, so stop trying to be everything. But there are things that we're all very, very good at and when we identify and embrace those things and they become the focus in our lives causing the feelings of unworthiness to take a back seat. Philippians 3 talks about focusing on one thing. I love that. How many of us focus on just one thing? Usually we strive to multi-task, focusing on many things at once and probably don't end up doing any of them super well. But Paul says, "We focus on one thing, forgetting the past and looking forward to what lies ahead.

I press on to reach the end of the race and receive the heavenly prize for which God through Christ Jesus is calling us." Now, you might say, "Hang on a minute, you told me to go back and deal with childhood hurt." Yeah, you have to, but you don't have to stay there. What I'm saying is go back, do what you need to, allow God to reveal and heal and then move forward. We don't stay in the past once we've dealt with it. That's not to say that the past won't come up again from time to time, but the objective is to deal with it so we can move forward with our lives. The other day something came up from the past, I took it to God straight away, we did business about it. I became free from it and started moving forward again. Don't stay in the past, look forward and then you'll move forward.

Philippians 3 says, "press on" not "skip on" or "float on" but "press on" because there is going to be resistance. Resistance will come your way, from other people and from those meanie little voices in your head. Press on to the goal to which God is calling you. Jesus said that His nourishment comes from doing the will of God who sent Him and for finishing His work. When He talked about nourishment, it was not in reference to food and the reality of food, but nourishment that comes from beyond the physical domain. Nourishment comes from

Don't stay in the past, look forward and then you'll move forward.

knowing the will of God, knowing our strengths and knowing what He's called us to. When we set goals and live within the boundaries we are nurtured and become alive.

Proverbs 16:3 reminds us to commit our actions to the Lord and our plans will succeed. It's about spending that time with God. Before writing down my life plan, I spent time fasting and praying because I didn't want to write "my" life plan because that would be rubbish. I wanted the life plan that God had assigned to emerge. When we begin by committing ourselves to the Lord and His plans, we'll see success in what we're doing and feel a sense of value, worth and achievement that pushes us on to greater and bigger things.

Proverbs 4:20-27 says, "My child, pay attention to what I say, listen carefully to my words, don't lose sight of them, let them penetrate deep into your heart, for they bring a life to those who find them, the word of God, and when He speaks to us, brings a life to those who hear them and it brings healing to the whole body." How much do we know that? "Guard your heart above all else for it determines the course of your life." It is so valuable to guard our hearts, to capture them as Christ's truth and spend time with Him when we've been in a situation that has deeply wounded, angered or offended us. "Avoid all perverse talks, stay away from corrupt speech,

Spending time with God is critical to determining direction in our lives.

look straight ahead". Once again, that reminder to look ahead and fix our eyes on what lies before us, fixing our eyes forward, marking out a path for our feet and staying on the safe path. Don't be side tracked, don't compare, don't try to please other people and live up to their expectations and keep your feet away from following evil.

How incredible is it that we should carefully listen to the words, allow them to settle in our hearts and then guard our heart against the enemy who wants to steal, kill and destroy. Keeping on that path and not straying to the left or right is where our success will come from. And this is a constant conversation that we will have with God, not a one-time sit down to offload everything. We're on a journey of continually seeking Him and getting our portion for the day. That's why our quiet time, the time we spend in the word and in prayer, focused on God and meditating on His word are so critical. That's where the food comes from and the wisdom and instruction that strengthens us for the journey ahead.

Goals, plans and healthy habits keep us moving forward and give us this incredible opportunity to celebrate life and discover what we're actually made of, or in God's case made for. As our plans align with Him there is much fruit to reap. We all want to contribute to life, and more than anything

I'm Enough

know that our life was valuable and meant something. I learnt an interesting thing about helping grow self-worth by having a self-esteem autobiography. It was about having a journal where you write down what's happening in your life when you're feeling good, when you're feeling empowered, valuable and worthwhile, because that's what you want to keep doing. And also writing down what's happening in your world when you feel worthless and struggle to find your value. Identifying those things will give you power and wisdom to help you as you move forward, and a big part of that is having goals and healthy habits and making sure you are moving in the direction that God has carved out for you.

Planning for the Future

Now is the *Time* to overcome self doubt and reclaim your *Value* and worth.

Taking Action

1. Set aside some time to pray about your future.

2. List the areas in life that are important to you – God, family, marriage, career, health, education, etc.

3. Ask God what His plans are for you in each area and write them down.

4. Now plan out what you need to be doing to achieve those goals. Try to focus on 3 or 4 at a time so you're not overwhelmed.

I'm Enough

Conclusion

We often went to Mandurah for our school holidays. In those days, it was a sleepy seaside town. Nowadays it is a thriving mini city that many have made their home. It was a chance to relax and get away. The only reason we could do this was due to the generosity of a family in our church who set up their tent in the local caravan park. They would vacate their tent for a week or so to give our family a chance to holiday there. Then they'd return to pack the tent away for another year. As we got older my brother moved away so only my mum and I went to stay there.

On one of these visits I met a boy: I can't even remember his name. We used to ride around the caravan park and chat. I was so excited that a boy was interested in me. One evening he asked me to meet him down at the caravan playground. I felt very grown-up for a 13-year-old, and with a mixture of excitement and fear I ventured out to meet him. All my friends had experienced their first kiss and a whole lot more, but at the ripe old age of 13, I had never before been kissed. We met at the park and talked for a while, but because there were other kids at the park he suggested we move away for some privacy. It was there that I experienced my first kiss, but what I thought was going to be a magical moment to share with my girlfriends turned out to be a nightmare. As soon as we were in the shadows, he pushed me down on the ground and sexually assaulted me. A mixture of shock, confusion and shame washed over me as I lay there paralysed with fear. For many years I didn't even acknowledge the horror of that event because I felt I deserved what happened to me. After all, what good 13-year-old girl meets a guy in the park at night? I must have asked for it.

I am so passionate about you knowing your true worth and value, because when you don't it makes you vulnerable to the actions of others. It will cause you to endure things you shouldn't have to, believing it's what you deserve. It will make you keep quiet, cover things up and ignore things that need to be brought into the light. It will also make you carry the blame for the shameful actions of others. That is not okay! We have been created in the image of God and His word says that we have been fearfully and wonderfully made. Even

Conclusion

more than the birds of the air and the lilies of the valley, God cares and tends to us.

We live in a world where women are taught to accept things. Fortunately, more and more people are starting to realise this and taking a stance against the unacceptable treatment of women. Now, I'm not going to get all political, but I want you to understand that it all starts with knowing our true identity and discovering our destiny on this earth. I want you to not only learn this and benefit from it, I want you to share it with your daughters, sisters and friends so that they may also know the life-giving freedom that comes from knowing your worth. No-one else can do this – it needs to be driven by us and for us.

In 1997, Max Lucardo wrote a children's book titled "You Are Special". It told the story of a group of circus performers called the Wemmicks. In between doing circus tricks the Wemmicks spent their time assessing one another to see if they measured up. If they did something well they got a star sticker and if they didn't do something well they got a dot sticker. The story centred around a lovable character named Punchinello who had lots of dots. One day he saw a Wemmick who was unlike any he had ever seen before. Her name was Lucia. Not only did Lucia have no dots, she didn't

I'm Enough

have any stars either. In fact, the stars that others tried to stick on her just fell to the floor. Punchinello befriended Lucia and she shared with him the reason nothing stuck to her. It was because every day Lucia went to Eli, the carpenter who made her, and as she spent time with him, Eli told her who she was truly made to be, so that the opinion of others did not stick to her.

We need to follow in Lucia's footsteps and spend time with our Maker to discover who we truly are. We need that truth to sink deep into our hearts so that when situations arise or others tell us we're not enough, it simply won't stick. I wish I could tell you that you can do things once and then never have to worry about them again, but as long as there are meanies in the world we will continually have to go back to our Maker to remind us of the truth. It's a process we will have to undertake for the rest of our lives, and one that will allow our lives to flourish. We'll feel lighter and won't be swayed by the tides of life, we'll remain steadfast and focussed, filled with confidence in what God has in store for us and how much He values us. Doesn't that sound like a great place to be? I would much rather be on this journey to freedom than spend another minute believing those self-defeating lies. Like anything new it will take time and sometimes it will feel

Conclusion

like we're taking two steps forward and one step back... but we will be moving forward.

The wonderful thing about this journey is that we don't have to do it on our own. God is with us all the way and has equipped us with everything we need to journey well. We will not only know how much He loves us, but be filled to overflowing with His love. It is with that love we will be able to bless others and free them from the trap of unworthiness, while those who love us cheer us on. They also want to see us free and flourishing. I wish I could give you a single solution that will forever cure your feelings of unworthiness, but it just doesn't work that way. The journey to knowing our true value and worth is lived out through an entire lifetime with God.

In Galatians 5:1 Paul says Christ has set us free, so stand firm and do not be burdened again by the yoke of slavery. Placing our worth and value in the hands of others is a form of slavery because we are handing over the power to others to determine who we are. Who are they to do that? Christ came so that we might have freedom and life in abundance, but it's up to us to grab it with both hands and run with it.

One day Punchinello got up the courage to go and visit Eli the carpenter. As he sat with Eli he dared to believe this might actually work and his spirits lifted as he thought about a life free from the dots. As Punchinello considered Eli's words one dot fell to the floor and his journey began. When will your journey begin? Do you dare to believe that what we've spoken about might actually work? Does your spirit soar as you contemplate life unburdened by feelings of not being enough? What would your life look like if you truly believed in what God says about you?

I think I just heard a dot drop ...

Conclusion

Notes

Chapter One: Eating Leaves

1. "The things that happen to us as children have a huge impact on our lives." Video 1, How to help deeply internalised hurt. NICABM. 2020. NICABM - Psychotherapy & Psychology Online Training. https://www.nicabm.com.
2. "King David" 1 Samuel 16:1-13, 1 Samuel 17:12-51.
3. "Maximus Decimus Meridius". Gladiator, 2000. Great movie, pretty gory but you get to see Russel Crow in a skirt! Ridley Scott, Scott Free Productions, 01 May 2000.
4. "When a parent doesn't value our temperament and tries to change us or expects us to performance a certain level, this causes damage and feeds those feelings of not being enough." Video 9, How to help your clients Internalise positive experiences. NICABM. 2020. NICABM - Psychotherapy & Psychology Online Training. https://www.nicabm.com.
5. "Studies have shown conditional love at an early age one of the greatest contributors to feelings of unworthiness." Video 11, How to help clients reframe their 'Never good enough' narrative. NICABM. 2020. NICABM - Psychotherapy & Psychology Online Training. https://www.nicabm.com.

Chapter Two: Falling into Crevices

6. "Jesus Baptism", Matthew 3:13-17, Mark 1:9-11, Luke 3:21-22.
7. "Wonder Woman", TV Series 1975-1979. Cool outfit, loved the lasso. Stanley Ralph Ross, United States: Warner Bros, Television.
8. "The expectations of others can drive us to impress them and do things we normally wouldn't do." Video 15 One exercise to shift clients out of a self-judging mindset. NICABM. 2020. NICABM - Psychotherapy & Psychology Online Training. https://www.nicabm.com.
9. "The advent of social media has brought with it a high expectation of people." Video 7 How to resource clients against toxic self-judgement. NICABM. 2020. NICABM - Psychotherapy & Psychology Online Training. https://www.nicabm.com.

Chapter Three: Gym Junkie

10. "Gideon", Judges 6-7
11. "Wheat Threshing." The bible Knowledge Commentary, Dallas Theological Seminary, Zuck, Roy B, Walvoord, John F. Judges 6:11-12b
12. "Elijah" 1 Kings 18:20-40, 19:1-18
13. "What we do not confront will not change" Bevere, J., 1995. Breaking the Power of Intimidation. 1st ed. Florida: Charisma House.

Chapter Four: Talking to Myself

14. "Moses". Exodus 3:1-22
15. "After thinking something for an extended period od time thoughts become automatic and we stop questioning whether or not they are right or wrong." Video 2. 3 Ways to overcome a sense of worthlessness. NICABM. 2020. NICABM -

Psychotherapy & Psychology Online Training. https://www.nicabm.com. [Accessed 04 August 2020].
16. "Strengths Test" Gallup, Inc.. 2020. CliftonStrengths Online Talent Assessment | EN - Gallup . https://www.gallup.com/cliftonstrengths/en/252137/home.aspx.
17. "Negative self-talk is one of the biggest contributors to not feeling enough." Video 10 The way a CBT practitioner works with negative core beliefs. NICABM. 2020. NICABM - Psychotherapy & Psychology Online Training. https://www.nicabm.com.
18. "Whatever you focus on expands" HuffPost, Verizon Media. 2020. Available at: https://www.huffpost.com/entry/whatever-you-focus-on-exp_b_3300091.

Chapter Five: My Time in the Sunshine

19. "Kasey Chambers", Not Pretty Enough. Nash Chambers, 14 January 2002, EMI.
20. "Shrek". Shrek, 2001. Andrew Adamson, Vicky Jenson, Dreamworks. A good laugh worth a watch, pay close attention to Donkey!
21. "Sigourney Weaver." Alien, 1979, Ridley Scott, United States: 20th Century Fox. Warning it is part of an epic series and is not for the faint hearted. If jump scares freak you out don't watch it)
22. "Baskin and Robbins", A highly recommended super cool ice cream and milkshake store!
23. "Goodyear Blimp". A cultural reference to the famous advertising blimps used by Goodyear Rubber Company from 1925 to today. https://en.wikipedia.org/wiki/Goodyear_Blimp
24. "At the age a child begins schooling their problem-solving development begins."Video 1 How to help deeply internalised hurt. NICABM - Psychotherapy & Psychology Online Training. https://www.nicabm.com.
25. "Adam and Eve - Garden", Genesis 2:15-19
26. "Nemo", Finding Nemo, 2003. Andrew Stanton, United States: Walt Disney Pictures and Pixar Animation Studios.

27. "Moana", Moana, 2016. Ron Clements, John Musker, United States: Walt Disney Studios Motion Pictures.
28. "Comparison." Video 7 How to rescue clients against toxic self judgement. NICABM. 2020. NICABM - Psychotherapy & Psychology Online Training. https://www.nicabm.com.

Chapter Six: The Addams Family

29. "Addams family" The Addams Family, 1964. David Levy, United States: Filmways Television, MGM Television. This show is creepy and kooky but to be fair it does warn you of that in the intro!
30. "Brady Bunch", The Brady Bunch, 1969. Sherwood Schwartz, United States: Redwood Productions, Paramount Television, CBS Television. The best series ever!

Chapter Seven: Survival

31. "Jesus Baptism" Matthew 3:13-17, Mark 1:9-11, Luke 3:21-22
32. "A lot of us a plagued by perfectionism." Video 13 How to approach unrealistic expectations of perfection.
33. NICABM. 2020. NICABM - Psychotherapy & Psychology Online Training. https://www.nicabm.com
34. Laura Daigle, You Say
35. "You Say" Daigle, L. (2018). You Say. Jason Ingram, Paul Mabury.

Chapter Eight: Leaving Kids Behind

36. "Psychologists use a term called 'Self Compassion' and define it as one of the keys to overcoming feelings of unworthiness." Video 5 How to repair attachment theory that fosters self loathing. NICABM. 2020. NICABM - Psychotherapy & Psychology Online Training. https://www.nicabm.com.

37. "El Woods, Legally Blonde", Legally Blonde, 2001. Robert Luketic, United States: Marc Platt Productions Metro-Goldwyn-Mayer. For all gals who love pretty pink things!

Chapter Nine: Ready, Steady, Go!

38. "David and Goliath" 1 Samuel 17:12-51
39. "Jonah" Jonah 1-4
40. "Levi Lusko" Lusko, L., 2018. I Declare War. 1st ed. Nashville. Thomas Nelson Publishing. (great book. A must read)
41. "Ash Barty", Ash Barty claims world number one spot after victory at Birmingham Classic - ABC News. 2020. Available at: https://www.abc.net.au/news/2019-06-23/ash-barty-claims-tennis-world-number-one-spot/11239490.
42. "It's all about Team Barty, says Ash" Roland-Garros - The 2020 Roland-Garros Tournament official site. 2020. Available at: https://www.rolandgarros.com/en-us/article/all-about-team-barty-says-ash-roland-garros.

Chapter Ten: Hearing Voices

43. "Studies show that we think faster than we speak." Dr Phil. Not even joking. I assume he learnt it from all the studying he's done.
44. "Levi Lusko- Naming the negative voice in your head", Lusko, L., 2018. I Declare War. 1st ed. Nashville. Thomas Nelson Publishing. Worth saying again, great book, a must read.
45. "Naming and identifying negative self-talk." Video 12 How to re-wire the critical mind. NICABM. 2020. NICABM - Psychotherapy & Psychology Online Training. https://www.nicabm.com.
46. "Xavier- X-Men" X-Men Series, 2000. Lauren Shuler Donna, Simon Kinberg, United States: Marvel Entertainment, 20th Century Fox. (fantastic series)

47. "If we believe people are not going to like us, certain behaviours and impressions that we subconsciously exhibit actually repel them." Video 6 How to help clients disengage from social comparison. NICABM. 2020. NICABM - Psychotherapy & Psychology Online Training. https://www.nicabm.com.

Chapter Eleven: Sticks and Stones

48. No References or Notes

Chapter Twelve: Planning for the Future

49. "Life plan" Hyatt, M. and Harkavy, D., 2016. Living Forward. 1st ed. Grand Rapids Michigan: Baker Books.
50. "James Clear" , Clear, J., 2018. Atomic Habits. 1st ed. London Random House Business Books.
51. "Strengths Test", Gallup, Inc.. 2020. CliftonStrengths Online Talent Assessment | EN - Gallup . [ONLINE]
52. Available at: https://www.gallup.com/cliftonstrengths/en/252137/home.aspx.

Conclusion

53. "Max Lucardo" Lucardo, M., 1997. You Are Special. 1st ed. UK, Candle Books.

One dollar from every book sold will be donated to the Foxglove project. If you would like make a further donation to this charity, please go to their website listed below.

The Foxglove Project is a registered Australian charity supporting women living in poverty in the Developing World to find autonomy and self-sufficiency for themselves and their families. Foxglove initiatives are committed to being sustainable, accountable and empowering.

Foxglove has 3 projects registered for tax-deductible donations: Birds Nest India, Focus Cambodia, Grassroots Rwanda

Please visit their website and discover how you can become a Foxglove supporter.

website: foxgloveproject.com
facebook: @FoxgloveProject
instagram: foxgloveproject
email: email@foxgloveproject.com

The Foxglove Approach

It's easy to see the needs in our world: clean water, food security, sanitation, education...but it's difficult to identify how they can be addressed.

For decades, overseas aid has centred on Western generosity funding infrastructure and welfare support. But the returns have been far 'poorer' than expected; the gap has increased between the rich and the poor, and the poor have become poorer! We need to do something different.

Foxglove focuses on people development. Equipping & supporting people to provide for themselves. We work through in-country partners to identify a community's poorest people, and invite them into local Self Help Groups to find friendship, training, access to finances and start micro businesses. This is the beginning.

The Foxglove approach may be slower and external change less dramatic but it's sustainable. It empowers a woman and her community to pursue social, economic and political priorities that last a lifetime.

I'M ~~NOT~~ ENOUGH Journal

If we want to get real about dealing with our worth and value issues it is going to take some work. The great news is that we don't have to do it alone, we have the Holy Spirit to help us navigate.

The I'm Enough Journal is an opportunity for you to spend time with God and record your journey into freedom. There is plenty of room to journal, however you like, and there is also room to record your responses to the questions asked at the end of chapters 7-12 of the book I'm Enough.

What ever way you approach it this is your opportunity for reflection and revelation in the area of value and worth.

Remember it is for freedom Christ has set us free so let us no longer be enslaved to the lie of not being enough. Take your time and value this journey because it may just change your life!

Order your I'm Enough Journal at

www.abidingprovidence.com/shop

Abiding Providence
MINISTRIES

Abiding Providence is an on-line ministry with the desire to encourage you to grow in your relationship with God.

What does the name mean?

Abiding: to dwell or remain.

Providence: God's wisdom and love in caring for His creation.

In John 15, Jesus describes Himself as the true grapevine and His Father as the gardener. He explains that just as a branch cannot produce fruit if it is severed from the vine we cannot produce fruit if we don't abide (remain) in Him.

As we abide (stay closely connected to God) He leads us in wisdom and cares for us because He loves us so much.

Abiding Providence represents my heart for all who read my blog or listen to my radio episodes. I want to inspire, encourage and equip you to abide in God's providence.

www.abidingprovidence.com

Subscribe to keep updated on new posts.

What can you expect at www.abidingprovidence.com?

Inspiration: My desire is to open your eyes to things about God and faith that you have never thought of before. I want to motivate you to change and grow.

Encouragement: I believe that everyone deserves to be free. Christ has come to set us free (Galatians 5:1). I don't believe true heart change comes from a set of do's and don'ts. I believe true heart change comes from allowing God to work in our lives. So, I want to be your cheer squad, championing you along this journey.

Equipping: I don't want to write and speak fluff that makes you feel good in the moment. I want to give you the tools that will help you to move forward and succeed.

Honestly: I am going to be raw and honest with you. I am on a journey too and I am still trying to figure out how to live this out. My heart is that you will be able to learn from my experiences and grow.

Lots of Love,

Leanne Whitfield

WORDS OF LIFE
collection

The Words Of Life Collection is designed to give biblical truth to replace the lies we so easily believe.

The renewing of our mind does not happen by chance, we need to engage with the way we think about ourselves and choose to change our internal dialogue.

Each series includes 10 individual cards adorned with inspirational quotes created from scripture including biblical references on the back and a wooden block so that the cards can be easily displayed wherever you choose.

The Words of Life Collection also comes in a mobile app and with every purchase there is a free download of that series straight to your mobile device.

The Words of Life Collection is so much more that words on cards. It is a powerful tool in renewing hearts and minds by setting them free through the truth of God's word.

Order your collection at
www.abidingprovidence.com/shop

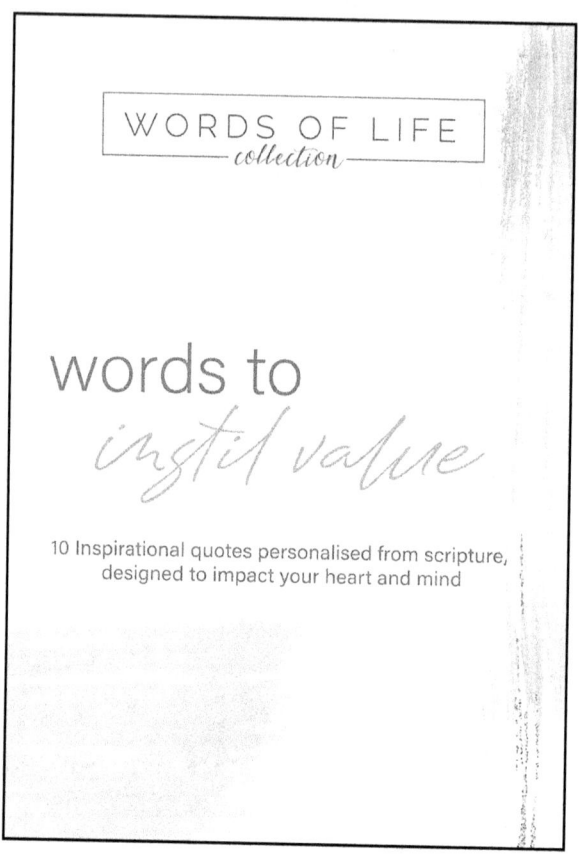

Adding to the Words of Life Collection range is "Words to Instil Value" This collection empowers you with the knowledge to overcome the feeling of not being enough with the revelation of your God given worth.

Words to Instil Value is a great companion to "I'm Enough: How to overcome doubt and reclaim your true value and worth".

The Words of Life Collections are so much more that words on cards. They are powerful tools in renewing hearts and minds by setting them free through the truth of God's word.

Available at
www.abidingprovidence.com/shop

STILL STANDING

I don't know about you, but my Christian walk has not been plain sailing! I have lost count of the ups and downs and twists and turns that have marked my journey. Just when it seems that I have traversed one challenge, another follows hot on its heels! Sometimes this leaves me feeling vulnerable and exhausted and other times I wonder which way to turn next.

I have looked at others and wondered if I am the only Christian who doesn't have it all together!

With the passing of time, I have recognised that certain strategies have helped me stand in the most challenging of times. It is these strategies I want to share with you. They have become my battle plan when everything is swirling around me and have helped me to stand and not be overcome.

You see, being able to stand does not come from living out of our own strength; it comes from standing strong because of our connection to God, the author of life (Philippians 4:12-13).

STILL STANDING is a battle plan that I hope will inspire you to stand strong and live a life that is intimately connected to God.

STILL STANDING is available as a free eBook when you subscribe to www.abidingprovidence.com or the paperback version is available at,

www.abidingprovidence.com/shop

Abundant Life Planner

I have come that they may have life, and that they may have it more abundantly.

John 10:10 (ESV)

I don't believe this abundant life that Jesus speaks of is one that is a crazy, flat out kind of lifestyle, constantly trying to cram more in. I believe Jesus is talking about a purposeful and fruitful life that includes things to do as well as space to breathe! A life that has Jesus at the forefront where our priorities and direction are guided by Him. An abundant life comes from seeking God, following His Word and passionately pursuing the calling He has placed on our life.

The Abundant Life Collection Planner is a quarterly planner and diary that will help you to be:

Fruitful: Keep on top of where and when things are happening with calendars and daily plans.

Focused: Being able to give energy and effort to the truly important things in life with clearly defined goals, weekly plans and quarterly reviews.

Flourishing: Process information into positive actions that improve with daily prayer, thanksgiving, sermon notes and weekly reviews.

Living Your Life to the Full

Available from Christmas 2022 at
www.abidingprovidence.com/shop

www.ingramcontent.com/pod-product-compliance
Lightning Source LLC
Chambersburg PA
CBHW050310010526
44107CB00055B/2175